ADULT ADOPTEE ANTHOLOGY

# Perpetual Child

### DISMANTLING THE STEREOTYPE

Edited and Compiled By
Amanda H.L. Transue-Woolston, BSW
&
Diane René Christian

*Perpetual Child: Adult Adoptee Anthology*
Edited and Compiled By: Amanda H.L. Transue-Woolston, BSW & Diane René Cristian

Individual writing copyright © 2013 by authors of respective work. All rights reserved.
First Print Edition: 2013

ISBN-13: 978-1492833444
ISBN-10: 1492833444

Cover and Formatting: Streetlight Graphics

# The An-Ya Project

*An-Ya and Her Diary: The Novel* (April, 2012)

*An-Ya and Her Diary: Reader & Parent Guide* (April, 2013)

*Perpetual Child: Adult Adoptee Anthology* (Winter, 2013)


For more information on the An-Ya Project visit:
www.anyadiary.com

*Working to dismantle adultism that keeps young people powerless and infantilized means sharing power with the young. It also means fighting patronizing adultist views that try to keep all adoptees in a child-like state as Perpetual Children.*

John Raible (August 2011)

*I'm not invisible I'm right here*
*I'm not a child; you don't have to speak for me*
*I will be counted, you can count on me*
*I will be here, are you listening to me*
*To me...*

From *Invisible* by Jared Rehberg
*(Lyrics written as a dedication*
*to Gazillion Voices)*

*And I can feel. I have learned to be "real" in the midst of pain. I can even, for the first time, sense the joy of realness, which makes some of the pain bearable. I walk stiffly, feeling like half-doll, half-person in the land of the living. Discovering my own humanity.*

\- Samantha Franklin

# Dedication

———◦✕◦———

*Dear Readers,*

THE MINUTE THE BLOG CHINESEADOPTEE.COM POSTED that *An-Ya and Her* by *Diary,* by Diane René Christian, and the accompanying adoptee written volume, *An-Ya: Reader and Parental Guide* were available on Amazon, I picked up the phone, credit card in hand and ordered both.

Two days later, nestled in a comfy armchair, I contemplated the beautifully designed, evocative cover featuring a pensive Chinese adolescent dressed in jeans, one foot awkwardly resting on a pile of stones, gazing wistfully far off into the distance. I read *An-Ya and Her Diary* in one sitting, captivated by the author's profound understanding of the firestorm of conflicting emotions an adopted child can face, her keen observations, grounded I hazard to suggest in experience: the sense of loss, not belonging, clinging to the increasingly tenuous bond with the past, aching for, yet reluctant to accept love, undergoing a whole gamut of emotions from rage, sadness, depression, guilt, to sparks of hope.

Christian captures it all, including the voids, which as adult adoptees, we all carry within but, if fortunate and resilient, learn to accept, honor and surround with tenderness and compassion. More than one passage reduced me to tears due to unexpected triggers that exposed an unacknowledged layer, buried at the core.

An-Ya is a fictional character but so lifelike that she springs from the pages of her diary as a vibrant child whom I will always carry in my heart. Her story is haunting, wrenching yet also full of hope for a joyous future, which I trust readers who embrace her as I have, will create and achieve in their own lives.

Though An-Ya will forever remain 12, like a character in Pirandello, immortal but immutable, she has moved me to contribute to the An-Ya Project's next much anticipated collaborative publication, *Perpetual Child: Adult Adoptee Anthology*. I offer these perspectives from my personal experience in appreciation for the cathartic tears and healing insights inspired by an exquisite book.

*Perpetual Child: Adult Adoptee Anthology, Dismantling the Stereotype*, gives voice with rich nuance to the infinitely complex universe of feelings, reflections and ongoing emotional conflicts that accompany us as adult adoptees in a life-long process. Our attempts to unravel, reassemble, identify and claim our sense of self in the face of widespread assumptions, we encounter from early childhood and well beyond, are poignantly and powerfully revealed through the gift of words that follow.


-Mei-Mei Akwai Ellerman

# Table of Contents

# Amanda H.L. Transue-Woolston

## DISCOVERING MY IMPOSED AGE & THE EFFECTS OF THE INSTITUTIONALIZATION OF PERPETUAL CHILDHOOD

I LOOKED UP AT THE CLOCK. Its second hand painstakingly ticked its way around signaling a fresh new minute. Nervousness filled the air as class prepared to begin. It was presentation day; we were to complete a twenty minute presentation on ourselves that demonstrated critical self-evaluation skills and self-awareness. While other students pondered what awkward or even painful disclosures they might make, I jittered excitedly in my seat because this project was a "do-over" for me.

Indeed, I had completed a similar assignment a few years prior when working on my psychology degree. I had stood in front of that class and all but horrified everyone as I began my history with a blank PowerPoint slide. "This was the day I was born," I said. "I was born without a name on a day I cannot tell you anything about. This was the start of my history—an empty slide." I had donned an *I'm fine with it* attitude and went about the presentation, blinking only once when I saw compassion and sorrow fill my professor's face. I suppose I had demonstrated that I was not very self-aware.

Now, was my chance to tell my story over again in an informed and empowered way. I could tell my beginning history because I now knew it and knew that it was not empty. During the previous year, I reunited with my original family, unsealed by birth and adoption records, and connected with my original family history for as far back as a genealogist could find. My birth narrative was not a blank space. It was filled with love and sadness and a real, tangible family. And yes, I did have a birth name. This presentation was the opportunity to put into words the integrative process I just experienced, and to put forth a confident *Self* I was proud of.

I looked down at the crisp white sheets in my hands; papers that contained the printed version of my slideshow. I designed my slides with white backgrounds so that the most colorful photographs of my life I could find would brightly shine from the screen. I sensed someone's gaze floating across my arm; I turned to meet the eyes of the classmate sitting next to me. "Hey, can I see those?" she asked. I shrugged and handed them to her. I watched as she scanned the pages while mumbling, "oh," "neat," and "oh cool" to herself. I saw her eyes stop on the "adopted" slide, and she did not continue on. She looked up at me, her expression changed, patronizing. She smiled and stretched her arm out towards me. I could not fathom what she was reaching for until I felt the tips of her fingers pat the top of my head three times. "I had no idea you were adopted" she said as though she were speaking to a basket of month-old puppies. "That is so incredibly cute!" She finished with a squeal.

I felt shocked and frozen; my mouth was fixed open revealing my state of stupor. If I had a mirror to look into I would have not been surprised were I to find myself transformed into a child. In my mind, I was the awkward 5th grade picture day version of me, complete with a pearl white beaded bow and a pink cotton dress with a lace Peter Pan collar. *What had just happened?* It was then that I realized that being adopted gave me an imposed age. I am a perpetual child.

That moment jarringly informed so many of my experiences involving my role as an adoptee when I had not been taken seriously and I could not fathom as to why. As my mind connected this meaning of "perpetual child" to these memories, it halted on a vision of me gripping the phone months back while the confidential intermediary broke my spirit into a thousand pieces.

Embarrassment and anger filled my chest as my mind vividly held this memory. I had waited for an unfathomably long time for the intermediary to connect me to my original mother. Unable to tolerate the silence any longer, I called to request an update. My inquiry was not greeted warmly. I tried to appeal to our shared humanity; I asked the intermediary to understand how terrible it felt for me to be stuck at the bottom of her pile of paperwork. This bureaucracy, this red tape, was suffocating me. She uttered dryly, "Well, not everything can favor the adoptee here." I felt defeated and something else I could not define until my peer patted the top of my head. *I felt like a child.*

I delivered the presentation that day with the rose colored glasses that had given me the idea that my adopted self would be universally accepted in the empowered way I saw myself knocked clear off of my face. My delight to be able to share changed into determination to be understood. I went home from class with a question in my mind; *do people really see me as a child because I am adopted?*

I embarked on a quest to understand why this happened to me; I needed to know what about being adopted made me a child in the eyes of some people. In the months following, I was thankful to find other adopted people writing on the topic of being treated as children, or youth adoptees being discounted because they are still children. The work of Dr. John Raible on the topic of adultism and parentalism was particularly meaningful to me in my own dismantling of this stereotype.

We tend to think of "ageism" as involving prejudice and biases against individuals of advanced age. Know that age-related bias and oppression also exist at the other end of the lifespan. In the U.S., our society values children in an abstract and charitable sense. We are prone to support organizations and policies that protect children, yet society at large harbors child-intolerant attitudes. We tend not to view the ideas and feelings of children and adolescents as being as important as those of their parents and other adults.

This translates into adoption when society forgets that adopted children become adults and when society treats adult adoptees the way children and adolescents are treated. We are asked to follow laws and policies that we did not help create. We are largely not given a place at the table in the discussion of adoption or in the creation of laws and policies. I once shocked my physician when I referred to myself as an "adult adoptee" and informed him I was keynoting a film festival that week. "Adult adoptee?" he pondered. "I suppose you're right. I do physicals on prospective adoptive parents all the time when they adopt children. I guess I never imagined those children all grown-up."

What does viewing adult adoptees as children have to do with policy? They influence each other. The attitude toward being adopted reflected in my "head patting" moment reflects the same attitudes policy makers harbor when they enact policies that do not take into consideration the needs and strengths of adult adoptees. The attitude reflected by my confidential intermediary was influenced by the policy she was required to follow; a policy that regarded me as a perpetual child.

According to Tennessee law, I cannot access my original birth certificate unless I have permission from my original mother. This portion of law pertains specifically to me because of my conception circumstances. In order to actually receive the record, I had to agree never to contact any person named in that record without permission from the Tennessee government. This "contact veto" process permits an original mother to prohibit contact with anyone she is related to, even if those individuals wish to speak to the adoptee. If these conditions were not infantilizing enough, the law clearly stated that if I made contact without clearance from the intermediary, I would face criminal and civil penalties. In other words, adoptees are assumed dangerous and volatile—completely incapable of respecting interpersonal boundaries unless preemptively threatened with the loss of their livelihood and freedom. This is a blatant institutionalization of perpetual childhood.

Once I spoke out about my experience with my birth state, I began receiving emails demanding I "leave well enough alone." I was called ignorant and ungrateful; didn't I know that this law is better than in some other states? What I experienced was called "good enough" for adoptees, or so I was told. I could not accept this. I did not become an adoption activist because I believe that adoptees need special rights over others in the adoption constellation (also known as "triad"). I simply ask for our dignity and humanity—and that of the children who will walk in our shoes—to be honored in every law made. I know that I must stand against the perpetual childhood stereotype to do this.

*Being a Perpetual Child is like being placed into a*

*container that is too tall to climb out of.* It is extensively listing your qualifications when testifying on adoption legislation and later finding the transcript with your credentials erased and qualified as a "personal story." *You feel the container come down around you. But it is too late; you have been dismissed to the children's table like Thanksgiving dinner at your aunt's house when you were six.* It is reading through bill deliberations on the law you wish to change and counting the word "child" used thirty-five times in reference to adult adoptees. *You are not being quiet in your container; that is just so "angsty" of you.* It is connecting to your first family and having an adoptive loved one remind you, "You know your parents adopted you because they could not have kids." *What to do now? Do you keep railing against this invisible confine or do you slump against its walls and give in?* It is the countless journalists who ask you to play your original mother's ventriloquist rather than speak from your professional knowledge. *Sit down. Be quiet. Remember, you speak from a rare and personal experience—you do not represent anyone else.*

Those who have viewed and treated adult adoptees as children do not necessarily do so to be intentionally dismissive, microaggressive, or hurtful. We were adopted as children; we were indeed once children. The key is for allies of adoptees, anyone claiming to care for adoptee welfare, to continuously work to check their own subconscious biases. This container does not have to exist. Adopted people can—and will—dismantle this stereotype and leave it in the dust. Yet we should not have to do it alone. Ending the perpetual childhood stereotype first begins with investigating the way that we view the feelings and ideas of children. It continues by working to avoid assigning those stereotyped child-roles to adults—in this case adult adoptees. It becomes effective when allies employ compassion, understanding, and self-awareness when interacting with adult adoptees. Change is slow, but rest assured, it will come. The children walking in our shoes who are embarking on adulthood are counting on it.

---

*the concept of elements of identity being "imposed" inspired by Susan Harris O'Connor's racial identity model.

# Nicky Sa-eun Schildkraut

## Everyone Loves An Orphan

*But I'm not an orphan,*
you said too late. They took you in,
anyway, unclothed and washed
you. As you looked around,
bewildered by all the others
like you, their mouths washed
to a silent pink as the nuns
said, *suck on this,* and gave you
each a candy, hard enough
to make your teeth grow
in crooked, you said, *But I know—*

your voice is not a voice
yet, only a noise of distress—
but here, they feed you. There
they read you to sleep. Here they
comfort you until you feel

washed clean, licked away.
Everywhere, love. Elsewhere,
a lily field distraction.

Later, it's clear what's
occurred: a natural disaster.
A hurricane beyond prediction.
Before that, a tragic epidemic.
No one says: your mother was kept
mistress to a married man,
or your mother stitched together
garments, day after day, until
her body bore a tiny, invisible
machine. Or, worse,
that your father was the other
man, who couldn't trade
his debt to save you though
he saved your brother. Or,
what if none of this
occurred? What if
you grew up in a strange
land, in a familiar family,
and you find out
everything was a deception, even
the history of the fact
you were born as an *orphan,*

a tiny machine
born from a field of weeds
they later called lilies, the nuns
bottling the scent of a sticky sweet
candy that boiled your mouth
and dyed your teeth and tongue
a wilted white?

*I know*— you start to say —
but they hush you to sleep,
closing the book with all
the words you can't decipher
as real words, yet, *you'll learn
another language.* In your sleep,
you're already talking
to yourself, filling in
the rest of the story.
*Once upon a time,*
*there lived a family...*

# Lynn Grubb

## Mother May I?

THERE IS A CENTRAL THEME in my life. It is like the game "Mother May I?" Here is how it is played: I am the perpetual child and I get to ask authorities (the government, the adoption agency and even my mother) if it is OK for me to know myself. Any information I am allowed to know about myself depends solely on the good will and decisions of my mother, social workers and government employees, all of whom get to possess my information instead of me.

**Step 1**

Ask the adoption agency for scraps of information (also referred to as non-identifying information). Hope to understand where you came from, but be grateful for little pieces of information that look like this:

"was 5'4" with brown hair and blue eyes"
"had an older brother and younger sister"
"her mother was a homemaker"
"Protestant"
"artistic"

*Take two steps forward and three steps back.*

## Step 2

Process the realization that your mother has never made any contact with the adoption agency she used to place you even though it is now 25 years after the fact. Confront the reality that your birth information is top secret. Decide there must be something really wrong with you if this is a secret.

*Go two steps back.*

## Step 3

Sign up for the state adoption registry and *hope* your mother is also signing up for the same registry. Wait. Wait a really long time. Wait forever. Realize she must not really want to see you if she is not contacting the last place she left you. You get no information (medical history, original birth certificate) unless your mother signs up for the registry and approves of this.

*Take one step forward and two steps back.*

## Step 4

Decide to petition the Court of your adoption for access to your Court file. For good measure, throw in your adopted mother's signature, so the Judge realizes that even though you are 38 years old, your adoptive mother "approves" of this decision. The Judge responds by denying said petition.

*Take one step forward and two steps back.*

**Step 5**

Realize that you are almost 40 and still do not know your mother's name, your father's name, your place of birth and the government is holding all your documents but refuses to give them to you. Realize that you are similar to Peter Pan in that you can never grow up according to the authorities inside the adoption world.

*Take one step forward and two steps back.*

**Step 6**

Pay your adoption agency more money than you would pay for anything else in your life (besides college) to search for your mother. Listen to the social worker tell you that you by law, she cannot reveal what state your mother lives in, or anything "identifying" about her. Realize that you just forked over a lot of money and if Mother says No, you will be put in permanent Time Out.

If Mother says yes, you win the grand prize: Her name.

**Step 7**

Your Mother says— Yes. Feeling triumphant, you ask Mother who your Father is. You are told he is somebody not worth knowing. A bad man. And she doesn't know his name.

*Take five steps forward and two steps back.*

**Step 8**

Send DNA samples to DNA matching databases and hope for a close relative match to your Father. Discover your closest match is also an adoptee with falsified records.

*Take two steps forward and two steps back to
genealogical purgatory... and stay there.*

Mother represents all that is nurturing. All that is love. She is the Goddess of protection. She is food, shelter and safety. Mother is idolized. She is Martha Stewart and Carol Brady wrapped into one.

My mother was different. She made a decision when I was pre-verbal to look at me through the glass of the hospital nursery, to pack her suitcase and leave. She never came back.

I know that my mother did not hold me. I was not nurtured at my mother's breast, nor did I feel her breath on my face. Mother to me represents pain, abandonment. Mothers leave.

We can call it a "loving choice" or "a desperate decision". To my tiny baby-self—it was rejection in its purest form.

In that act of leaving, Mother not only took away her maternal love, she took away my ancestors, and my connection to me. Now I continue to play the game to try to win back all that I lost.

*One step at a time.*

# Karen Pickell

## THE LETTER
### (A STORY)

I'M GOING TO THE POST office today. I'm going to mail the letter. It's on my nightstand in a long white envelope, already stamped. My name and address are small in the corner, and yours is front and center, written large in my neatest hand. Lynda Tanner. "Lynda." I say it out loud in the shower.

I search my closet for the right thing to wear, something comfortable, not too flashy. Something cool enough that I won't sweat. I find a cardigan, pinch the sleeve to gauge its heft, decide it's just right to pair with my denim capris and leather sandals. The sun is strong today. Trees have their flowers, and flowers have bees.

The post office is a short drive away. I could drop the letter in the box outside, roll down my window and lean out to let it fall in, never leave my car. But what if I miss the box somehow and don't see the envelope fall to the ground? What if I run it over with my own tires, then it blows away or a squirrel runs off with it and it ends up stuck in the clump of decaying leaves caught by the fence, rotting, festering. No, I'll park and take the letter inside.

On this crisp, white rectangle, you'll see how I slant my letters, how I write in halting cursive that breaks into moments of childish printing, that loops and swirls yet is firm and at times unyielding. You'll see a different state in my address and it won't make sense. Will you even open it, or will you toss it in the trash with the other junk mail? I could send it certified, require you to sign for it, but then you'd have to be home to receive it, and if you weren't home, would you go to your post office to retrieve a letter from someone you don't know, from a state you might have never visited? Then again, if I just send it like a holiday card, I'll never be sure you got it.

This folded and glued bit of nothing more than paper holds my longing of thirty-seven years. I wrote the letter on fine stationery with a lace-like design embossed in the margins. I put down the words longhand, in my best handwriting. I used my favorite pen, a Paper Mate stick pen with black ink, because my writing flows best from its smooth-rolling ballpoint. I needed to be at my best. It took me all night, a whole life, to write the letter. Now it's folded in thirds inside this envelope with your name across the front.

I remember when the search angel told me your name over the phone—"Lynda," a name I'd used for my dolls as a child, though in my mind it was spelled differently because I have a cousin named Linda. It's a name I've always liked. I tried to figure out what the name told me about you. I pictured someone kind and pretty. In Spanish, "linda" means pretty, but I know you're not Hispanic. I've seen myself every day in the mirror. Maybe you were named after an ancestor or a character from a book your mother was reading. The name doesn't tell me anything. But it makes you real. It gives you shape and a whole life I know nothing about. You're not mine anymore. You're out of my imagination and out in the physical world, in Michigan, near Detroit and the lake.

I've looked up your address, seen the shadow of the building where you live via satellite courtesy of Google maps. I wonder if you were cooking dinner inside when the shot was taken. You might have been at work though. I found your cosmetology license on another website. When I was young, I was the one who styled the hair of all the girls in the neighborhood, so we have that in common. I even briefly considered becoming a professional stylist myself, but that was more like a fantasy than a real ambition. It's strange to think that wanting to do hair could be in the blood. Maybe it's related to wanting to be pretty.

I picture you as pretty, because I've seen your signature. The search angel sent me a copy of your marriage license. Your "Lynda" is large and round, the kind of cursive that's obviously feminine and intent on grabbing attention. It says LOOK AT ME. Or, maybe it simply says *see me*, an eighteen-year-old girl trying to be a woman. I wonder who he is, if he's my father, this Mr. Tanner. Your divorce decree mentions custody of two daughters. Do they know about me? They would be out of your house by now.

I don't have your phone number, but even if I did I wouldn't call. I would be too afraid that you'd hang up on me, or that you'd yell or even worse, cry. I would sob, I know that. I'd have to read from a script and then I'd probably mess that up. I'm better at writing. I could have typed the letter, but I wanted you to see my handwriting, to feel my hands on the paper. When you hold the pages between your fingers, the oil from my skin will touch yours and we will once again be connected. You'll have to know then that I'm real and that I'm yours. But if you have any doubt, dust the paper for my fingerprints. I've licked the adhesive on the envelope's flap to seal it tight, included a spit sample of my DNA you're welcome to analyze.

I should eat before I drive to the post office. I skipped breakfast this morning and now I feel weak. It's a perfect day, not a cloud to be seen. I wish a late winter storm would dump sleet and hail all over the roads, but we don't get storms like that down here even in the winter. I wish the tornado sirens would sound. It wouldn't be safe to drive with a tornado approaching.

I'm just being silly now, letting my insecurity grow wild. I put the stamp on the envelope last night, when I decided I would go to the post office today. I have some bills to mail, too, so I need to go today. If I don't go, they'll be late. I don't like leaving bills in my box here at home for the mailman to pick up. Someone might take them out and get hold of my account numbers. No one would want my sappy letter, but how would a thief know that's all it was? Then I'd have to write the letter all over again and I don't want to do that.

It took a half hour just to figure out the salutation. "Dear Ms. Tanner" was, of course, too formal; "Dear Mom" was out of the question. I went with "Dear Lynda." I hope I'll come off as warm and friendly and not psychotic.

Then I had to introduce myself: *I was born on June 2, 1968, in Detroit, Michigan, and subsequently adopted. I'm writing to you because I believe you might be my mother.* Whether or not you'll read what follows is anyone's guess. Maybe you'll stop right there, tear the whole thing into shreds and light it with a match, so that no one will ever find out and you can continue to live as though you have two daughters rather than three. But we do have the hair thing in common. Maybe we have other things in common, too, like needing to know the truth or needing to know our family. I can't believe you would just forget about your first child. I haven't forgotten about you. I have to assume you're like me and will want to know more, so you'll read the rest of the letter.

That's assuming you get the mail on the day it arrives. Maybe you live with someone—a lover, a friend, one of your children. What if someone else gets the mail? What if the someone else is suspicious of why you're getting a letter from out of state and opens it himself, learns you have another child you never told him about? What if he thinks it's junk and throws it out with the other meaningless solicitations that clog the mailbox? Hell, you might even toss it away with the junk yourself. You won't recognize my name. It's not the one you gave me.

The search angel found that name on my birth record, along with yours. I wasn't just "Baby Girl." I have to think that means something, that you cared for me. Why would you name me if you didn't care for me? You must wonder what happened to me.

But you never looked for me. I know that. I've been all over the message boards and the registries, and I've never seen one post looking for a baby girl born on June 2, 1968, in Detroit. If you were searching, I would have found your messages. The agency would have a record of you contacting them. They don't. Why haven't you looked for me? I thought you'd find me once I turned eighteen, then twenty-one. I waited for my phone to ring with your call, but it never did. No letter arrived. I waited as long as I could stand to, and then I decided to look for you, to do the work myself. Maybe it isn't fair that I know so much about you now when you know nothing about me. Maybe you want to be left alone, but it's too late because I've found you and now I have to let you know that I'm here. But what if I ruin your life? What if you never told anyone about me and I crack your world open? There's no way for me to know how you've lived your life after giving me up. I don't know you, and you don't know me.

I have this letter to mail to a stranger, you, the woman who gave me life. I wrote down a synopsis of my childhood and my present life for you, so you would know that I've been okay and that I don't need anything from you other than to hear why I am and why it had to be this way. I need to know if I should worry about breast cancer or glaucoma or some rare condition I've never heard of. I don't need you to take care of me. I'm not a kid anymore. I've been taking care of myself since before I became an adult. I don't need you to mother me.

But that's a lie, because I want you to wrap me in your arms and stroke my hair. I want to find out if I remember your smell. I was once inside your body. Now I'm sending you a letter, ink on paper, biodegradable. One day it will be dust, as will we both, and none of this will matter, except to the descendants of my children, your grandchildren, our legacy. They'll want to know—don't you think?—about where they began. I'd like to know how our people came to be in America, if they came from Ireland or Germany or someplace else. I'd like to know what branch of humanity I fell from. I'd like to know how your parents felt about losing their granddaughter. Of course, maybe it's their fault to begin with.

I know things were different back in the '60s, that young, single mothers weren't accepted the way they are now. I grew up Catholic, too, so I know that you broke some big rules and that your parents were probably very upset with you. Maybe you didn't have a choice. I remember when I was a teenager trying to imagine what it would be like to have a baby of my own, trying to figure out how I would take care of it if I didn't have my parents' help. I don't know if I could have done it. I understand why you couldn't do it.

It's important that you know that I'm not mad at you. I put that in the letter. I hope you won't be afraid to answer me because you think I'll be angry. I'm not angry with you. But I wish things could have been different.

The kids will be home soon. I'd better go. If I don't get to the post office in the next hour, I won't be able to make it today. I have to get there today.

I'm going to the post office now. My purse is on the passenger seat. The bills are piled next to it, and the letter is on top. At a red light, I glance at it and read your name again. *Lynda Tanner*. My mother. I'm going to mail a letter to my mother. This is the day.

The parking lot is half full. I find a spot across from the door to the post office. The air is warming now that the sun has been high for over an hour. Birds are making their new nests in the big old trees. I walk in slow motion across the asphalt, my hand gripping the bills and the letter.

When I open the door to the post office, the customers notice me, the clerks notice me. The neurons under my skin are shooting sparks. I feel like I am jumping, unable to keep myself in order. My eyes look from face to face. The people see all my energy. How could they not? They know something big is happening. They recognize the panic I project. The yuppie guy checking his P.O. Box turns to look at me, smiles. He knows. I'm here to do something I'm not supposed to do. Contacting you, knowing where you are, knowing your name—it's all forbidden. That's why I had to hire a search angel to be my private investigator, to sneak around in the records of my birth and the documents chronicling your scant interactions with public authority. These people in the post office have an instinct about me, like the one I get about certain people when I ride public transportation, a sixth sense that warns when someone is up to no good.

But they mind their own business and let me be. I cross the room and stand before the slot for stamped mail. I separate the bills from the long white envelope bearing your name, easily push the bills into the slot. Blood is in my ears and I can't hear the conversations around me.

I am in the post office. I am going to mail the letter. It is rattling in my hand. I visualize it falling behind the wall into a bin filled with hundreds of envelopes; a man dressed in blue sorting it with the mail bound for Michigan; a white truck carrying the bag containing the letter; a jet landing in Detroit; another truck, another post office; another man driving a small white truck, leaning out to pass the letter from his hand into your mailbox; your hand ripping the envelope, the one that my hand holds right now.

My hand pushed a pen across the pages inside this envelope, made words with ink for you to read, to tell you about me, that I am here, that I am real. I shed my skin on the pages, the dust poured inside the envelope; shards so miniscule they'll fall onto your shoe unnoticed when you pull out the letter. Maybe you'll see some of them floating in the sunlight coming through your window. No, you'll get the mail in the evening, after work, when the sun is low, when the sun has gone. You'll carry my letter inside with the tiresome ads and your bills—another payment requested, but this one in blood and tears. What right do I have to ask you for anything? You did what was best for me.

My chest is shaking. I hold the corner of the envelope just inside the slot. I only need to give it a push, to let it fall from my hand and behind the wall, into the bin. I don't have to do it. I can drop the letter in the trash bin behind me instead, walk back out to the car, drive back to my life the way it is, the way it's always been. I have my own family. Why do I need this? I am a grown woman, not a little girl, not the baby you gave up. I have my own babies. I know how their skin smells. Yet some nights, after I put them to bed, I can't stop my tears from coming, and I know I'm feeling sorry for myself, for everything I missed. I want to shake myself out of this self-pity. I want to not feel like a child anymore. Will contacting you make it any better?

I pull the envelope back, read your name again. "Lynda Tanner." You are my mother and you are real. I didn't fall out of the sky. I was born from your belly, just like my babies were born from mine. You felt me moving inside you. You fed me from your body. I'm an intelligent person, I understand biology, I know intellectually that I was created by the coming together of two people, my parents, but I never felt like I came from another person's body until I learned your name. I have a mother just like everyone else's mother and her name is Lynda Tanner. Someday my children won't live with me in my house. I won't hold them every day the way I do now. They will move to another street, another city, another state. How will it feel to not have them physically near me? I can't imagine not feeling connected to them. I know that whenever we visit each other, I'll pull them right back into my arms. I don't know if you held me after I was born. Maybe you didn't. But I lived inside you for nine months. I feel connected to you, and I have to believe you still feel that connection, too.

I'm here, at the post office, standing in front of the mail slot, and I'm going to mail my letter to you. I turn the envelope over in my hand, raise it to my lips, and gently brush it with a kiss. I slide the edge of the envelope into the slot, flick it with my finger, and hear it fall into the bin filled with countless envelopes behind the wall.

I try to swallow, but my throat is thick. I'm tingling, like every hair on my body is standing on end in fear. I make it out to the car, grip the steering wheel, and stare out the window at a bird flitting between branches of a huge old tree silhouetted against the bright spring sky. I wait for your reply.

# Catana Tully

EXCERPTS FROM *SPLIT AT THE ROOT:*
*A MEMOIR OF LOVE AND LOST IDENTITY*

## *I've lived over half a century*

**Pumpkin Patch Baby**
*January 1995*

I T WAS MID DECEMBER 1994. The first winter storm in the Northeast left a slick, icy, carpet. Trees glistened in the sunlight; the world was quiet, clean, and cold, and the season had people hustling in preparation for the holidays.

Winter invariably rekindles childhood memories - this year begging to appease the urge to be with Ruth. I had left Guatemala eight months before, knowing full well I'd have to see her again soon. In the course of a recent phone conversation, she told me of a dream where she was driving in a car with Mutti and five other friends who had all passed to the other side. "Tell me," she said sounding a bit aggravated, "what am I doing with all those dead people in my car who are constantly scolding me and telling me what to do?"

A nervous chill ran down my spine when I heard that. Could they be telling Ruth to come clean with me and fill in the details she's been avoiding? Oh horror, are the dead perhaps coming to claim her? A deep sense of sadness came over me. I knew so little about Mutti's daughter; I should know more about the woman who lathered my body with baby oil so I'd grow up having soft skin. She clipped and creamed my fingernails and toenails. My teeth are straight, thanks to Ruth who helped me massage the gums each morning, who drove me to the dentist and paid my dental bills. She played with me, read me stories at night and taught me prayers. I made all those countless wishes with her at my side. The thought of her dying was unbearable. I needed to be with Ruth and tap into the reservoir of her perfect memory; she was my childhood haven, my security.

I booked a flight for December 29th. That way I'd spend the holidays with my men, and visit Ruth for a few weeks before spring semester began.

I'm in Catalina, sitting at the desk where I used to do my homework, going over the list of questions I need to have answered. I'll sleep again in the bed where I curled up as a child. My clothes are in the closet where my girlhood dresses hung; my shoes on the same old shoe rack. This room is my cocoon where I can retrace my steps, become younger again; feel protected, invulnerable. Ruth is here, my room is here: I feel safe. A few hours ago I heard her on the phone saying to the Lutheran minister, "My sister Catana arrived from New York. It's only when she's here I feel the family is complete." I've been part of this family all my life, and yet, why does it touch me to tears when Ruth includes me today? Is it because I never wanted to return after Mutti passed? Or because there had been such bad blood long ago? Mutti and Rudolf, the cornerstones of discord, were out of the picture. Ruth and I were left behind to mend the fences. We were Mutti's daughters, after all. We were sisters who had at one point loved and hated, only to regain love for each other in old age.

It was during my first lunch that Ruth's six-year-old granddaughter confronted me. A brilliantly intelligent, but most inquisitive, and therefore rudest questioner imaginable.

"Where's your mother?" The fresh little face asked.

"She's dead, you know that. Ruth's mother is dead," I said, already sensing this might become uncomfortable.

"Not that one. I mean your mother, your **real** mother," her dark eyes pierced mine.

"She was my real mother," I answered unfazed... This was going to be a challenge.

"I mean your mother when you were born," the girl insisted, and everyone began to chew more slowly. Obviously, the kids had asked before and were given an answer. But that hadn't been enough for this little monster. She wanted *me* to say that my mother was so poor she couldn't take care of me and gave me away. That way her great grandmother and grandmother (and by extension, she) were magnanimous heroes to whom I should forever be indebted.

I wasn't going to be bullied into telling a little kid things I myself was, as yet, incapable of understanding. So, I offered her the story of the big leaf on the river. She was quiet while she played with the peas on her plate. Then, with a little crooked I-know-the-real-story smile, she said:

"Who was the woman who gave birth to you, and then put you on the leaf to float down the river?" Her smile was pretty condescending for a six year old.

"I was a miracle," I said patiently.

Her eyes flashed poisoned daggers at me; she was losing her patience with so much stupidity. "Everybody's born from a woman," she contended defiantly.

"I can't help it," I shrugged and calmly added, "That's the story I was told."

"That's not the way things happen... And, she wasn't your mother!" The little dragon voiced triumphantly.

"You mean to tell me that your grandmother told me lies?" I blinked a few times as if shocked at the possibility.

Her eyes softened as she looked at Ruth, not sure if she should say her grandmother was a liar. After all, she knew about babies being born: her pediatrician father had allowed no room for flights of fantasy.

"No," she mumbled, a bit uncertain. "My granny tells the truth." She chose a diplomatic solution and began to eat her mashed potatoes.

The ensuing conversation among the adults was a bit forced.

Suddenly, the high-pitched voice rang out again: "You," the young inquisitor said pointing her index finger at me, her pretty face beaming broadly, "are a cabbage patch baby!"

Thanks to American enterprise, her scientific mind had allowed for imagination, after all. Children are born, but cabbage patch babies... are probably left on big leaves.

"You're going to be a brilliant scientist," I beamed at her.

"Nope," she answered resolutely, "I'm going to be a doctor, like my dad."

"When I was little and told my story," I said to her and the other children at the table, "all the kids were jealous because they were born in a boring sterile hospital, and I had floated down a river on a big jungle leaf," I shrugged, smiling.

"Well," she replied, looking at her father. "It's just that today everyone knows how babies are born."

"Now really," I said giving her dad an admonishing look, "you, of all people should know what babies are," I laughed.

He grinned, and winking at the children concurred: "Absolutely, all babies are remarkable, wonderful miracles."

With that, the questioner remained quiet. From time to time, she looked at me out the corner of her eyes, but she got it: from me, the answer she wanted was not forthcoming.

This sort of situation had tormented me throughout my life: I was unable to ward off unwelcome interrogation. I couldn't tell people the personal questions they asked me were none of their damned business. I answered as truthfully as I could even though I felt thoroughly invaded and miserable at my breached boundaries. Those asking came across as having the authority to know. This little girl was only six, but whether six or sixty, questions about the birth mother are insensitive to a child who did not grow up with her. Somehow, natural children (and adults, too, mind you) set out to make adopted ones feel inferior. Our birth mother is not as good as theirs, because we did not grow up with her.

I had a cramped feeling in my stomach and ate little at that lunch, but having worked through it, I was pleased as pie to have crossed that threshold. I would never again be pushed into that uncomfortable place.

### Things Start to Unravel

*I stand motionless atop a rugged cliff, scanning a landscape where a cloudless sky spans the horizon. The jasmine-scented breeze touches the tassel hanging from my cap and dances in the folds of my gown... Yes, my gown, my newly acquired heavy black silk academic regalia. Three velvet stripes on the sleeves honor the doctoral degree, and the blue, gold, and white striped hood lying on my shoulders represents the School of Humanities. "Here they are," I hear the breeze whisper in my ear, "time for you to try them on." I turn my head to the right, and from the corner of my eye see a majestic wing, the sort a renaissance artist would have pinned on the Archangel Gabriel. "There's one on the other side as well," the breeze adds jokingly. I would hope so, I think to myself, and smile. "They are light but powerful, Catana; it's time for you to use them." I hesitate. "Go ahead, go now." Tentatively, I hunch my shoulders forward, then upward; I spread first one, then the other wing. I look again to the right, then to the left and carefully move the pair of magnificent extensions. "They're perfect," the breeze murmurs, "now fly..." Obediently, I flap my wings once, twice, and the wind lifts me up. "Courage," the breeze calls, sensing my fears. "By the way, you look like a natural at this. Good luck," I hear as the wind carries me onward and upward, and I soar like an eagle. Like an eagle I dip and glide weightlessly, but purposefully in the air. I survey the immensity of what lays before, below, beside me. Mountains, hills, valleys, I glide through canyons and ravines, skim over streams and lakes, over sandy coastlines, and up again to hover above snow-capped mountains: inhaling the breathtaking splendor that surrounds me. Suddenly, unexpectedly and uncalled for, the glorious wings collapse spectacularly and I spiral downward from the heavens, out of control, like a dejected angel.*

I awake frightened, disoriented, and bathed in cold sweat.

After six years of focused academic work, I completed my doctorate in Humanistic Studies in 1989. Following my advisor's suggestion I applied for an academic position at a college nearby.

The dean was duly impressed by my credentials and

after the interview called his assistant requesting she make the necessary arrangements for me to meet the team of interviewing faculty.

A friendly Black woman with kind eyes and a relaxing, motherly quality escorted me to her office where she offered me a seat in a chair across from her desk. She picked up my résumé, read it with interest and studying me, said: "Nowhere in this Vita do I get the sense that I am reading about a Black person." I was stunned by her comment and explained that my degree was in the Humanities, broadly speaking. Instantly, I began to worry that she had discovered something important the dean had missed.

"It's all very interesting and interdisciplinary, of course," she said in an easy manner, "but you don't show studies that deal with Black issues."

"I'm Hispanic," I answered too rapidly for my liking, "and my high-school education took place in Jamaica; I have a British high-school diploma, and have studied and worked in Europe for many years." A nasty sense of discomfort began to engulf me. Why was I explaining anything at all to this assistant? What business of hers was it anyway? She was Black and I already knew what she was about to do. She, like all Black people, was not going to accept me as one of her own, and in spite of her friendly demeanor, she intended to put me down.

"Why don't you join a Black professional organization?" she suggested. "That would make it clear to everyone that you are Black... on paper as well as off."

I sighed with relief and thanked her for the suggestion. She was right, the obvious should be reflected in my Vita: as an educated older woman, Hispanic, of African descent, I was a valuable multiple minority, the sort colleges were desirous to employ. The woman had only been helpful and friendly, when I was ready to assume the worst. I had hoped to land a job before I was fifty, and I succeeded, for I was forty-nine years and eight months old when I signed the contract. That was early 1990. I would turn 50 in August.

What had happened? What had the panic in the assistant's office been about? Why had I been riddled with insecurities? Again? No matter how much I'd been commended for my work, I still worried I'd do or say something asinine and blow it. What was it that caused such inner turmoil, such a debilitating feeling of inadequacy? I had not only done well, I had done great! After all my hard work, I should be at a place of inner peace and comfort. I had been a successful actress; had landed parts when they were few and far between for people like me. Same thing with my career as a model; I worked almost all the time. In Mexico, where I taught myself to paint behind glass, my paintings sold the day I left them at the gallery. And now, after very few years, I completed an academic career I was deservedly proud of. That should be enough reassurance, right? This should not have happened again.

But it did. What a let down! And I can't tell any of my friends about these debilitating circumstances for, as always, as far as they're concerned, I've lived my entire life in the best of all worlds.

I had been there before: a grown woman reduced by her ignorance of self, and fear to have that lack of self-knowledge discovered. Would I ever be able to leave the raw vulnerability of a lost child behind me? Will the early indoctrinations ever release my psyche and become a woman to fulfill her full potential?

## Meeting my Birth Father Gil

It sounds odd for sure, but I never thought about my conception. Not even in the back of my mind. Being Mutti's cherub, fallen from heaven onto a mound of grass, was so much more appealing than owing my existence to two people having had sex. Even as I held my baby in my arms, it did not occur to me to think of how or when the spark was ignited that brought me into this world.

That Gil had been a married man when he conceived me started to intrigue me. Here I was, the product of a secret, passionate love affair — the sort one reads about in romance novels, where lovers are drawn together by an irresistible force. I was the result of bashful stolen glances, whispered longings, tingling fingers, secret places... Perhaps they conceived me on an afternoon when torrential downpours trapped them in a moss-covered grotto. Perhaps, on the sultry sands of a coral beach, my father embraced my mother under a canopy of trembling stars. Two young brown bodies fused into each other, embraced in forbidden passion must have created me.

What would Gil see when he looked at me, I wondered? Would my lips, as I shaped them into words and smiles, take his thoughts back to long forgotten embraces? Would my skin remind him of the texture of my mother's velvet body? Could looking at my eyes rekindle the spark that lit his soul? In how many ways would I remind him of my mother, the woman he had secretly held in his heart?

I drove to Brooklyn to meet my father on a gloriously sunny June day in 1992. Along the freeway, pines, maples, elms, and birch trees boasted shiny new green. Here, bushes of wild pink and mauve rhododendrons; there, yellow forsythias were in full bloom. Patches of white wild flowers dotted the hillsides, and the Catskills seemed more beautiful than I had ever seen them. I was at peace as I raced south on the New York Thruway, over the Tappanzee Bridge, down Henry Hudson Parkway, through the Brooklyn Battery Tunnel, along Shore Parkway, to the Rockaway exit. I made the various turns I was instructed to take and ended up on a tree-lined street in a courtyard with poplars. I parked next to an elegant, white American car and walked to the building thinking: Brooklyn? This sure is a lot better than I had anticipated. A doorman announced my arrival. The elevator took me to the fourth floor, and I walked to the end of the corridor to apartment 4B.

After bracing myself with a slow deep breath, I raised my hand and rang the bell. The sound of footsteps behind the door made my heart pound so loudly I missed the shift of the latch. He's not six feet at all; he's my height, was my first thought. The hair he had in my photograph was gone. Before me stood a portly, pleasant-looking, elderly gentleman in a perfectly tailored medium blue linen suit, pale blue batiste shirt and a conservative, small print, dark blue tie. Elegant to boot. He was right: he could be taken for a successful doctor, lawyer, or businessman. I was the professor from upstate who had merely taken care to color-coordinate her clothes.

"You're punctual," he smiled mildly. "Did you have a good trip?" I felt his eyes absorbing me as he gestured for me to enter.

"Everything went very well. After all, I had excellent directions," I smiled at him and stepped into the strikingly clean apartment. The living room was to the right, but I was directed left, to the kitchen where Vivian sat at a table. The Haitian woman who came three days a week to stay with her while Gil ran errands was also there.

"Mrs. Tully," Gil said formally, "this is my wife, Mrs. Reed."

"How are you, Vivian? How are you feeling today?" No way was I getting stuck in formal shenanigans, and I handed her the box of truffles I brought for them.

Vivian's illness had reduced her to an ethereal whisper. A long tube attached to her delicate nose connected to a large oxygen tank. Having long lost the vibrancy of health, her eyes were but sad, opaque pools of pale grey. As I held her tiny breakable hand, I was overwhelmed with sympathy for her and wished I could make my strength flow into her body.

"Hello, Mrs. Tully," she said in a strong voice that defied frailness. Turning to Gil she exclaimed, "She looks exactly like Lucio!" And after looking me up and down, somewhat louder remarked, "It's amazing, she's Lucio all over."

"Who. Is. Lucio?" I asked.

"He's your uncle. He's Edmundo's brother, Lucio Cayetano," she explained.

"Interesting... I've never heard that name."

It was clear I had to get Gil away from Vivian, as she was set to control the content of the conversation. The plan was to meet at his home and then go somewhere to talk. He wasn't making the first move.

"We need to talk, Gil," I said, feeling quite brazen. "How about going for coffee somewhere?"

"Yes, of course," he obliged. I promised Vivian to visit with her later.

On the way out, Gil picked up a folder lying on a table by the entrance. Where'd I get the courage? How great was that! Yes! Without sitting down, I managed to extricate my father from the clutches of his wife.

I had indeed parked next to his car: the newest model of a fancy Chrysler. One glance at my Honda Civic, and Gil decided we'd take the Chrysler. It was immaculately clean, inside and out, and had every gadget that made travel comfortable, including a collection of cassettes with catchy dance tunes. This eighty-one year old geezer seemed to like fun and was prepared for pleasure. "Tell me what this is," he said placing a cassette in the player.

"Guatemalan Marimba," I shrugged.

"The whistle, listen..."

"And?"

"That's the sound of the Ferrocarril Verapaz in Livingston! Isn't it great?" His face beaming all over.

The whistle of the German-owned train that used to bring coffee from the highland plantations to be shipped to Europe had become part of a syncopated rhythm that invited to clap hands, tap feet and swing hips. I shook my head and grinned, as I recognized the makings of a troublemaker in my pedantic father's eyes.

"I want that table by the window," the hostess heard as he walked by her and she followed. It was, of course, the best table in the place, and he took the best seat. Then and there, it struck me that he behaved with the natural, uncomplicated, self-centeredness of a White man.

Sunlight filtered through the window softening our features as we sat facing each other. A faint touch of his cologne spiced our booth. I asked for coffee. "Nothing to eat? You've been on the road for hours," he noted, and ordered two coffees and two English muffins. No questions asked. My eyes followed his graceful gestures as he spoke to the waiter. "I don't feel like eating either," he gazed at me, "but you must eat something." I smiled amused at his paternal command.

"All right then, a muffin's fine," I agreed, grinning.

He was assertive, sure of himself... Quite a difference to the man he had been in the apartment. After a few pleasantries - he obviously wanted to get Mutti issues over with - Gil opened his folder. In it were various letters from Mutti (I didn't know they had corresponded for years), newspaper and magazine articles of my days as an actress in Germany, and several photos in various stages of my growing up.

With unnecessary flourish, he handed me Mutti's last letter dated 1955, the one that had prompted his irate response. She had written a little about me and quickly came to the point: she needed his authorization so I could leave Guatemala and study in Jamaica. "Now Gil, I want you to tend to this matter immediately. Don't you be lazy and let time go by! Make sure you take care of it right away." I was shocked at the tone... so unlike Mutti. Apparently she saw no need for any formality on her part. Now Gil, do this; don't be lazy, do it now... Wow, no respect! Had the letter been typewritten, I would have sworn on any Bible that it wasn't Mutti's. Then he handed me with visible pride, a carbon copy of the irate response he'd fired back. It was the letter that had finally gotten her off his back, for good. "There is no proof the girl is my daughter," it said, "and not until I am convinced of that fact will I move in any direction." Who knows who signed what, but I left Guatemala late August 1955.

I brought with me what little I had on Gil: my legalization, name change documents, and the old photo. "You signed the photo on the same date you signed my name change," I stared him down. That means you were in Guatemala on those dates. His shoulders sagged, and for a few seconds he seemed confused.

"It was rough for me then," he murmured. "A lot of people were trying to convince me of all sorts of things regarding you." His expression was grave. Up to that point in his existence, no one had curbed his carefree lifestyle.

"Whatever you have against Mutti, Gil, accusing her of bribery is not only unfair, it's a lie. After all, I resembled you." He looked up at me and I detected a flicker of acknowledgement in his eyes. "And Gil, what about your insinuation that she was in love with you... Did you have an affair with her?"

"Heavens, no! I said that the other day because my wife was right next to me. When it comes to this situation, Vivian turns my life into a living hell. I'd just as soon not upset her, being that she's so frail and all."

"Why did you keep my photos?"

He smiled, his voice husky, "I never really knew whether I was your father or not. But..." he paused smiling shyly, "now I know." His expression was priceless.

The maitre d' came by to greet us. "Well, Mr. Reed, you have a lovely young lady at your table this morning," he said in a rather smug voice.

Grinning broadly at me and winking, Gil answered spontaneously: "She's my daughter."

"I knew it!" The maitre d' said, "She looks exactly like you."

I smiled at my dad. We both knew.

After the maitre d' left Gil leaned toward me, like wanting to share a secret. "There's something you should know," he lowered his voice. "I was with your mother only once. And to tell the truth, I no longer remember when, nor where, nor how."

Once? Oh no... Once? Ohhh... Out the window flew my dream of being the fruit of passionate illicit love, of bringing back to old man memories of the one woman he had truly loved but couldn't have... Out, too, flew the fantasy of my father looking at me and remembering with tenderness, caresses he had exchanged with my mother. Turns out it was a single forgettable encounter, probably a kneetrembler that would hang over their heads and follow them like a nightmare for the rest of their lives. Suddenly, I began to laugh and so did he. If nowhere else, here we had to recognize ourselves in the other. We were cut from the same outrageous fabric, had the same shameless character. Someone else in this world did the same type of nutty things as I. But above all, the old man was sensuous. There was such masculine grace in the movement of his hands. His long, slender, delicate fingers ended in oval well-manicured nails. I couldn't remember ever seeing a more beautiful pair of hands on a man. Mr. Reed was funny and disarmingly charming: a man with distinct, self-centered mannerisms whose erect posture and easy movements had the touch of an aristocrat. I could certainly see women falling in love with this tidy well-cared-for man.

"After that one time," Gil murmured, "I never saw Rosa again. She didn't want to have anything to do with me. Every time I wanted to speak with her, to clear things up, she adamantly refused to see me," he whispered, shaking his head. After so many decades, he still looked lost when recalling a time when he was young and deeply conflicted.

"Why?" I wondered.

"I'll never know," he shrugged. "I suppose she must have loved Edmundo, and he'd give her hell if she talked to me."

"Why could Mutti have been so sure you were my father?"

A sly expression crossed over his lips. "That woman protected Rosa. Believe it or not, she never allowed your mother to go dancing. With me, she finally agreed." He kept a serious face but could not conceal the laughter emanating from his eyes.

"No!" I shrieked aghast.

"Yeah! Imagine," he grinned broadly, "I was the only one she trusted with her."

"How often d' you take her to the village?" I asked bemused.

"Once," he grinned.

Well... That's all it takes... Again I burst out laughing. I wiped tears from my eyes and cheeks... gasped for air and laughed until my stomach hurt; I just couldn't stop! Mutti! What was she thinking? She had delivered my young mother to the wolf, the village Lothario! And... there was no question about it: I was the man's daughter for he was laughing as out of control and shamefacedly as I.

"You were drunk, otherwise you'd remember," I finally stammered, gasping.

"Yes, I drank too much when I was young," he paused. "Gave it up long ago... But then, way too much," he shook his head, no longer amused.

"And what was your relationship with Vivian during that time?"

"I had a relationship with her, but didn't marry her until after my mother died in 1953."

Aha! I could see Mutti's mind working overtime. Gil was light in complexion and had a better future, so Mutti figured he'd be the best match for her Rosa... I could almost see how she instigated the whole thing; except it didn't work out the way she'd figured. The one single time she allowed Rosa out of her sight... That's why Mutti knew. Oh, geez, poor Rosa, she must have been sick with shame. Getting knocked up by a partying and drinking kind of guy... Who knows what she told Edmundo, but I was born looking like Gil.

I barely touched the muffin. I was too filled with emotion, admiration, and heaven knows what else to think of eating.

Gil led the way to the car. As he walked ahead of me I had a wild urge to tear his clothes off. I wanted to look at his body, wanted to see if his shape was like mine. Were his legs thin like mine? His feet narrow and delicate like his hands? His toes long and pretty? I observed how he gracefully placed his feet on the ground, how his trousers fell on his shoes. I had a very good inkling that my body looked like his, and from our behavior in the restaurant, I acted and reacted like him. There was no question, I was his daughter, and he knew I was his child.

Gil let Vivian know we were back but didn't ask her to join us. He directed me to the cream colored sofa in the living room and handed me a leather-bound photo album that had been on the coffee table. My father stood next to me, observing me as I studied the contents of the book. In it were two pictures of a young 'Old Man Reed,' dated 1887 and 1888, and taken in a studio in San Francisco, California. No wonder Mutti called him old: one of the portraits was taken the year of her birth. On the opposite page was a photograph of my grandmother, Liberia. Edward Reed, Liberia Espinoza: my grandparents. I examined the two dissimilar people: the conqueror and the conquered. Europe and Africa in America, I thought. Young Edward was even-featured and handsome in a nondescript way. His expression was cool, aloof, a little arrogant, as he looked into the camera. It was a typical pose of early photography. Liberia was already older when the picture was taken. Her face glowed in the sunlight and she looked tired as her large body relaxed into generous folds. She looked solid like a tropical Mother Earth. I sensed my father watching me as he introduced me to his parents. I looked up at him and found him gazing down at me, a deep absorbing expression in his eyes. What was it about my father's eyes? What was going through his mind when his attention was focused so absolutely on me? When I noticed his eyes burning on me, I fell deeply in love with Gil. I fell in love with his knowledge of himself and because he presented me with my heritage. Only then, when my childhood was long over, did I understand that I had missed not having grown up with him.

"Halloo... What are you talking about?" Vivian called from the kitchen.

I couldn't allow her into my magical morning and ruin it. Not making good on my promise to spend time with her, I got up and said I needed to get home. Gil walked me to my car and stood at the curb waving as I pulled away.

It was only 10:30 and I had accomplished much more than I had hoped for. I needed time to digest this spectacular morning. The drive, Brooklyn, Gil's immaculate apartment, Vivian attached to the oxygen tank saying I looked like someone I had never heard of, removing Gil from her clutches, the maitre d' confirming me as Gil's daughter, my less than memorable conception, and seeing photos of my grandparents, aunts and uncles. Above all, Gil's scorching gaze focused on me as I studied his parents. The phone rang as I stepped into my home three hours later. It was my father who wanted to make sure I had arrived well. Gil was in my life.

The next day I called him on the spur of the moment to declare my joy at having found him. Not surprised at my infatuation he responded in kind but then excused himself abruptly. Fifteen minutes later, I ran to the ringing phone. "Please don't call me again," he said hurriedly, "Vivian gets very upset when I talk to you. She's distraught that I didn't reject you. But how could I have, after seeing you?" I smiled and closed my eyes, as a warm feeling engulfed me. This is just wonderful I thought. "I'll call you from now on, on Sundays at noon. I love you," he whispered and hung up.

And so began my phase of writing tempestuous love letters. If I couldn't speak to my father, I would communicate with him in a way that would not be harmful to his wife's frail state.

*My darling, darling Gil,*

*I love the sound of your name, Gil, Gilberto. When I hear your voice on the phone or when I write to you, all I sense is profound adoration. I am infatuated with the love that flows between us. Papá, a word I have never said to anyone. It feels good to say it to you; to know you as my father. I want to understand so much, everything, about you. You are that part of me I ignore; and I know that through you I will come to recognize who I am.*

*What fascinates you about me is seeing that in me you continue into the future, and in me, too, you find your parents and all previous generations that carried your genes.*

*My son and my husband rejoice at your being in my life; and when your time and obligations free you up, we will all meet.*

*I embrace you tenderly with all my love and all the love you deserve. I kiss you, papá.*

*Your daughter who adores you,*

I don't know how he was handling things at home. He said he had become restless since meeting me; that Vivian was aware of it and knew the reason. We communicated in Spanish. English he called "the blunt language of economists and barbarians. Spanish, on the other hand," he declared, "is the language of lovers. Think of *corazoncito*, such a tender, loving word. But 'little heart?' that's a deformity! Makes me think of hospital, ambulance, emergency surgery. I write to you with the most tender sentiments of my *corazón*, my adored negrita."

*Negrita*, or darkie, is similar to Mutti's Mohrle. Had anyone ever dared to say *negrita* to me, I'd have been profoundly offended. Now, it came from Gil, from a Black man in whose eyes I was authentically beautiful because I was Black, because I was his. For the first time, *negrita* was a loving term. I became Gil's *negrita*, and could barely wait to read it in his letters, or hear the word from his lips. He wrote as often as I did: every second day.

I didn't even think to compare Gil with my German father who had been there when I was physically a child. Gil was there as I was a woman, a woman in need of being a child with her father who looked like her, was like her, wanted her and needed her as a daughter.

# Lucy Chau Lai-Tuen Sheen

## MUSINGS OF A TRANSRACIAL ADOPTEE

But there are times when I still feel like a
lost and lonely child

It happens less and less now

But there is inside me somewhere a little
corner of Neverland

In The Best Interests of The Child

I was prised away from the land of my
ancestors

With talk of rescue and salvation dripping
from Colonial lips

The lack of where-with-all, the superficial,
of far more import then

In The Best Interests of The Child

I was placed upon the school desk as the
subject of "bring and tell"

It was my Adoptive Mother who brought
and placed me upon the desk

Then told thirty Caucasian open wide cat
eyed school children who and what I was,

or should that be what I wasn't?

In The Best Interests of The Child

Clean break

Don't refer at all to where the child has come from

In The Best Interests of The Child

"She chatters away in her own little language"

The feeling back then, in swinging 60s UK

"It's probably best to knock that one on the head"

She's here in the UK now English is what she needs to be

That was something I was never going to be

But everyone swept that one under the carpet

It's a new life

A new country

I was a small baby

I was their China Doll

I was lost and I was losing

My language, my name, my heritage, my culture

I was like one of those nests of Russian dolls

The difference being there was nothing at my centre

I was empty

A ghost child hovering between two worlds

The one that I was displaced from

The one that I grew up in.

Maybe it's a coincidence that I do what I do now?

I "play" because the child that never was, is only now being allowed out to play?

I chose a profession where I take on different identities

Speak other people's words and feel other people's

emotions

Perhaps because I never truly was, has made me the actress/writer that I am?

The child wide eyed with wonder and fear still searching

But after half a century what am I still searching for?

# Laura Dennis

*AM* A PERPETUAL CHILD.

In many ways, it might not be such a bad thing.

Of course I'm not referring to the reality that I do in fact function as a wife, mother and colleague in the real world (whatever *that* is). I'm not talking about shirking my adult responsibilities as a fairly upstanding citizen—I pay my taxes, and I am a law-abiding citizen (for the most part).

I'm talking about the childhood attitudes that I had as an adoptee; beliefs which carry over into my adult life. Yes, in this sense I am—and continue to be, a perpetual child. But not in the fashion that some may assume.

Although the American White*, middle class, Judeo-Christian society in which I grew up would have been similar to the place I would have been raised had I not been adopted, this *particular* culture's mainstream view of adoption is that it is a positive, one-time occurrence in a child's life and nothing more. The narrative that once the adoption closes, the first mother "moves on" with her life, the adoptive parents get a baby that they raise as if it were their own, and the adoptee lives happily ever after, is widely accepted.

The subtext is that if the adoptee bristles at all against this perspective, he or she is an ungrateful adoptee, an angry adoptee, or both. Such suppositions on the part of this "adoption-positive" society turn into accusations, placing the adoptee in the role of defending herself, feeling belittled and misunderstood.

Accordingly, the adult adoptee is placed into the role of the perpetual child, and in that sense, it is an imminently frustrating position.

Today I'm here to tell you: It doesn't have to be that way.

## The "Perfect Child"

Growing up as a domestic adoptee in a closed adoption, I was quite determined not to be seen as a child. I took great pains to be considered mature and serious. After knowing me for the entire school year, teachers often commented that they never knew I had dimples. As June came along, if by chance an observant instructor happened to catch me in some rare unguarded moment in which I accidently let a smile emerge, he or she would inevitably delight in noticing my deep (and, it turns out, hereditary) dimples.

It's safe to say I was a child who had no need or interest in my childhood. From my four-foot tall grammar school vantage point, it was dirty, sweaty, and too loud.

Truly, I was the quintessential perfect child, the grateful and obedient adoptee. Even though my adoptive parents weren't strict or (too) dogmatic, I was constantly trying to figure out and even *anticipate* their expectations of me, just so I could meet and exceed them. I imagine I may have been a very exasperating child—having high demands on myself meant that I expected the same of others, especially my parents. I know my mother still regrets going out on a limb and purchasing one of those funny cards for one of my preteen birthdays. I was so offended; I always hated celebrating my birthday (little did I know that I share this in common with so many adoptees), and then here my mom goes and gives me a humorous card! To me, without the flowery background and sappy poems, it meant she didn't love me after all. My birthday was simply a joke to her. (Now you can see how high maintenance I really was.)

With this in mind, some might wonder if I thought about being adopted every day.

Do you think about the fact that you're a girl and not a boy every day? Or vice versa? Perhaps. More likely, it simply informs who you are at the very core of your being (whether you accept the gender/sex you were born with, or not). Adoption was not something I chose, just like I didn't choose to be a girl, or to be White, or to have these thick-boned thumbs that people suggest I have surgically thinned. (Some individuals have no verbal filter, clearly.)

Adoption was a decision made before I was born. It was a contract signed before I had a say. It was a transaction made, money exchanged for a newborn, White baby. *Tabula rasa* and all that.

But I'm getting a bit ahead of myself.

I grew up in a Judeo-Christian culture, specifically a Catholic family. My mother instilled in me a strong belief system, but acknowledged that we must ultimately be led by our own personal sense of morality, recognizing that the Pope is in fact a fallible human. My father, a brilliant mathematician, had a scientist's skepticism and, in my opinion, mostly went along with our Catholic upbringing for the sake of my mom. Together they taught me to think critically. And they shouldn't have been surprised when I began to think critically about adoption.

But of course, they were.

**Slavery, Adoption and Hamburgers**

One afternoon in Maryland in the late 1980s, after dutifully attending Mass, we were enjoying our customary meat-heavy Burger King lunch (I'm now a vegetarian, go figure). It was then that my ten-year-old thought-processes led me to question my parents about some aspects of adoption that I really wasn't buying.

In fourth grade Social Studies, we had a unit on pre-

Civil War plantation life in Maryland. We learned about the economic "benefits" of slavery (benefits only for wealthy non-slaves, that is). We schoolchildren were dutifully appalled at the notion of owning a person as property— the prospect of buying and selling humans abhorrent and difficult to fathom.

And yet, I could imagine it. I could imagine it very well, because I was living proof that a 400-year legacy of slavery in the United States was alive and thriving. Yet, no one seemed to think of it as such.

Which is why I asked my parents, How much did you pay the adoption agency to get me?

I don't quite remember the exact details of the conversation, but there was a pregnant pause (pun intended) and then some effort at clarification as to what exactly I meant. You see, my parents had always been very open about my adoptee status, forward-thinking in the fact that they told me I was adopted from when I was a baby, before I could even understand. They told me as much as they knew, repeating the fraught line so many adoptees have heard, "Your mother loved you enough to give you up, and now we love you."

Eventually they tried to explain, clarifying that they paid fees to the agency to *handle* the adoption, not to purchase me.

Armed with my precious fourth-grade education, I wasn't buying it. "Yes, but you paid money to get me, right?"

"Yes, we paid *fees* to the agency," my mom said, my dad nodding, uncharacteristically quiet.

"How much did you pay for me?"

P-a-u-s-e.

This was not what my parents signed up for. They thought they were getting a baby, a blank slate, whom they could raise *as if it was their own*, not some infant who grew into a fresh-mouthed kid, questioning her very existence in the family, wondering at her monetary worth.

Perhaps they chose their words carefully; perhaps it was the first thing that came to mind. It could generally be assumed that my parents were not the ones spending their evenings after we kids were in bed, pondering the best ways to explain the facts of life. More likely, my father was zoned out in front of the TV, and my mom was praying herself to sleep, hoping to be able to pay the bills for another week or so. In due course, Mom said, "The fees we paid were to cover the hospital costs for your birth."

No matter the thought involved, had I known about health insurance at that time (but heck, I was only ten), I would have called 'Shenanigans.' My birth mom came from an *upper* middle class white family, better-off in fact, than my adoptive family. She was a minor when I was born. Surely her parents had health insurance for her and her four older siblings.

Once I opened the door, I wasn't stopping. I asked, "How. Much?"

"We paid about $10,000. For your hospital fees, Laura!" Mom insisted.**

"You paid money for me; you bought me, like a slave."

After that, the direction of the conversation likely detoured in fervent hopes that I would forget about all of these crazy questions about adoption.

Of course, the critical thinking perpetual child in me did not stop pondering my adoptee status.

**Adoption, Slavery and ... Kidnapping**

I had seen pictures of the adoption agency my parents used, and had even returned there with them to "pick-up" my new baby brother. I was so proud at the age of five when I was allowed to be the first person in our adoptive family to hold him. Accordingly, even as a preschooler, I knew a bit about how one goes about "getting" a baby.

And I knew that money changed hands.

After all, a couple can't just walk into an agency that

has access to little babies, take one for your very own, and leave... without paying for him or her. If you don't pay and you take someone else's baby, well, we all know what that is... It's *kidnapping.*

This memory of picking up my brother, combined with the unit on slavery, only added to the "paying for a baby" idea I'd been contemplating.

But seriously. What does it really matter that my ten-year-old adoptee-self accused my adoptive parents of buying me, like a slave? After all, we all know that adoption is not exactly the same as slavery.

Very true. Yes, adoptee abuse exists, but the institutionalized enslavement of an entire race of people to build and sustain an economy is not the same thing as what happens in adoption. I get that. I know that I wasn't *enslaved* to my adoptive parents. Nevertheless, we can look at similarities in what Whites (and others) did to perpetrate slavery—to justify it and to integrate it into their culture and government—with what happens in modern adoption. The change in the American perception of slavery didn't happen overnight (I'm talking the general population, not ignorant, prejudiced outliers). The same is true for adoption as an institution.

The thing is that there will always be mothers who can't, or won't, take care of their children. There will be parents who are unfit, abusive and unsafe. While I don't agree that adoption ought to be outlawed, I do believe that it must be strictly regulated, with the exchange of money eliminated. Perhaps take out the middleman of adoption agencies and require families to work directly with social services, like foster care.

With any change in an institution, we must start with hearts and minds.

In slavery, one way that Whites justified their actions was by deciding that Blacks were sub-human and therefore unfit for freedom. We know today that slavery is wrong, and that it's absurd to argue that people with a different skin color than White are somehow inhuman. Yet at the time, this notion seemed perfectly reasonable to the general American population. Whites wanted to fit the people they enslaved into *their* paradigm, and other Whites went along with it. It would take time and education to overcome these perceptions.

In adoption, one way that adoptive parents and agencies justify their actions is by arguing that they are "saving" a child from a life of institutionalized care.

At the outset, there is nothing wrong with this statement. Who would want children languishing, ignored in an orphanage? Not me. But as we've learned from recent research projects such as Kathryn Joyce's *The Child Catchers, Rescue, Trafficking and the New Gospel of Adoption*, and from adoptees themselves, adoption is not a one-size-fits-all solution to "saving" a child. Even the widely accepted designation, "orphan," may be a misnomer; many children do have family, and have been placed in orphanages temporarily.

## Perpetuating Institutional Flaws

The connections drawn between slavery and adoption don't stop at "mere" moral justifications.

One aspect of adoption that I didn't quite understand as a child was the contractual nature of what occurred when my adoption papers were signed. At the close of my adoption, my legal ties were severed with my biological family, and reassigned to my adoptive one. Inheritance rights, name, access to medical records, health history and knowledge of bloodlines; all severed.

Adoption advocate, Lesley Jane Seymour, from *First Mother Forum* explains,

> But save slavery, there is no other contract in the world in which two parties (the birth/first mother and

*the state) enter into which so affects and controls the current and future status of a third party—the one who is adopted—without any input from her or him. The contract between the birth mother and the state destroys the legal and real identity of the individual in most states for all eternity. The contract does not have a term limit, nor can it be changed when the adopted individual becomes an adult. The state upholds the contract, considers it a legal document that must take precedence over any desires of the third party, the one about whom the contract was written. How is this not like slavery?*

An excellent question, indeed.

My perpetual child—both the very real ten-year-old and the metaphorical perpetual child that rises to the surface throughout an adoptee's adulthood, had no real understanding of the contractual nature of my adoption. To quote the ubiquitous Wikipedia, a contract

> is an agreement having a lawful object entered into voluntarily by two or more parties, each of whom intends to create one or more legal obligations between them. The elements of a contract are "offer" and "acceptance" by "competent persons" having legal capacity who exchange "consideration" to create "mutuality of obligation."

Ah ha. I see, now. "Offer" and "acceptance." In this case, the offer and acceptance are ... of a child. Adoption is a contract between two parties in which there exists a third party. A *person*. Specifically, the adoption contract is created between the relinquishing mother and the adoptive couple. (First fathers have little-to-no rights to their child in most U.S. states.) There is no party representing the child; the adoptive child has no say. With the court system in divorce and foster cases, at least there is a guardian appointed to represent the needs of the child. With the adoption system, no such representation on behalf of the child exists.

I had no say.

Adoptees had no say.

Adoptees still have no say.

I was adopted as a child, actually a baby. But I am still adopted, and I will continue to be adopted. For the rest of my life. As many of my adoptee friends like to point out, *we can't just wake-up tomorrow and poof! We're not adopted.*

I mentioned hearts-and-minds. Once we recognize the flaws inherent in adoption as an institution, one might wonder, *What can be done?* How can we change an institution in which the person at the very heart of the matter has no say?

Early on in this article, I made the distinction that I was raised in a White American culture that is adoption-positive. The reason I pointed this out is because as an adult, I've come to see that not all White cultures value adoption in the same way.

I recently moved to my husband's homeland, Serbia, where adoption is considered the absolute last resort for a child. (Serbs are Caucasian, hence my distinction that not all White cultures value adoption like the White culture in which I was raised in the United State.) International adoption is frowned upon—exactly *because* a child loses his ethnicity, language and cultural heritage. Money is not allowed to change hands in adoption and adoption agencies are not permitted to operate. As a result, yearly international adoptions have dwindled to less than ten— mostly older and special needs children. When adoption outside of the biological family happens, it is rare.

Change in adoption starts with changing the perception that it's what's best for the child. What's best for the child is family preservation in a home with a stable, capable biological family member. Adoption should exist; but as a last-case scenario.

In order to get to such an understanding, we must acknowledge that adoption involves loss. Perhaps it should not be outlawed as slavery was/is. Perhaps there will, sadly, always be instances in which a mother–given all the resources in the world—will want to relinquish her child to someone outside her or the father's biological family. Nevertheless, adoption should be the option of last resort.

As an adoptee, that fresh-mouthed, critically minded perpetual child is still there, too. (Some would call it snarky sarcasm, and I would consider such moniker a compliment.) Many in the adoptee community like to appropriate the terms "bastard," self-identifying as such because in reality, that's what we are (illegitimate), and there's no shame in having been born out-of-wedlock (we had no say in the matter). By claiming this, and other so-called derogatory terms, we can take away the stigma and stand proud.

Yes, I was adopted. Yes, I am *still* adopted, and I am *still* a perpetual child. Neither term defines me in a negative way, or in a comprehensive fashion. Rather, such an adoptee/perpetual child status is part of my famous/infamous "adoptee resilience." It causes me to continue to question institutions that don't make sense to me. And that's a good thing.

---

* I am capitalizing White to denote that just like other ethnicities, White or Caucasian is in fact an ethnicity with its own characteristics and values. Instead of naming "white" with lower-case, which assumes that "white" is the dominant narrative, I am using White, specifically in the case of my childhood—White American, to state that mine is just one of many ethnicities. It's important to note that I certainly am not a sociologist, nor an expert on the subject of race relations.

** Approximately thirty years later, the 2008 cost of a vaginal birth in New Jersey is $17,300. Even if my first mom hadn't had insurance in 1977 when I was born, $10,000 is an exorbitant amount to cover the hospital fees. My mother lived at home while pregnant, and spent only about 24-hours in the hospital. Clearly, the agency was making money off of the transaction.

# Julie Stromberg

## LET'S PRETEND

I LANDED MY FIRST PAYING, NON-BABYSITTING job at the age of 15. The Perrot Memorial Library in Old Greenwich, CT hired me as a page and sent me out into the stacks with a wooden, rolling cart piled high with returned books in need of reshelving. As a voracious reader, this was my dream assignment in a historic, local book-filled institution that I adored. And while I was a reliable employee, it was not unusual to find me in the library's dedicated Mystery Room "skimming" a novel that caught my eye from the cart of bibliophile temptation.

In order to work in Connecticut at the age of 15, I needed my parents to sign permission papers as I was under the legal working age of 16. The library also requested a copy of my birth certificate to verify my identity and citizenship. I did not yet have a driver's license so my birth certificate was the only option at the time. And I'll never forget the rush of emotion that came over my entire being after my mother retrieved my birth certificate from the bank's safe deposit box and presented it to me.

I almost missed the fact that my adoptive parents were listed as if they were my biological parents. My eyes immediately landed on information that, up until that point, had been unknown to me. I was born at Saint Francis Hospital in Hartford, CT at 9:37 p.m. and a doctor named Mary Kay Karpinski had delivered me. Strange as it may sound, it felt so odd to acknowledge that I had been born to someone and delivered by another someone in a hospital. I always knew that I was adopted. Yet up until that point, my personal history and life's narrative began with "and then we picked you up at Catholic Charities in Bridgeport when you were 2 months old."

After my stomach stopped flipping around a bit, I realized that my adoptive parents' names were typed in the spaces reserved for "Father of Child" and "Mother of Child." Their ages at the time of my birth and places of residence were also listed. It suddenly occurred to me that the entire document could be a lie and not just the part about my adoptive parents being my biological parents. If that information could be fabricated, I wondered, what about the city, hospital and doctor? Was the whole thing a total sham or just the parents part, I questioned. Why was I being forced to pretend that I was someone I could never be—the biological child of my adoptive parents?

Sham or not, I immediately wanted to run down to the Old Greenwich train station and hop the next Metro North and Amtrak to Hartford. I desperately wanted to find Mary Kay Karpinski, MD so that I could ask her if she remembered being there when I was born–and if she remembered my first mother. I actually had the name of someone who could possibly tell me what I so very much needed to know about myself. Where had I come from? Who had I come from? Who was I? I had to find this doctor and ask her. I needed to be released from this game of Let's Pretend that I never agreed to play.

I kept all of those feelings to myself, however, and instead dutifully took my amended birth certificate to the library and offered it as proof of who I was—all the while thinking that it was really proof of who I wasn't. I never was, and never would be, born of my adoptive parents. I suddenly felt as though there was something wrong with being adopted and that being a part of an adoptive family was somehow shameful. Why else would I be forced to use a document that made our family appear to be something it could never be?

At the time, I was unaware that there was a factual certificate of my birth and that Connecticut had made this document inaccessible to me–as well as those belonging to all adoptees born in the state–just before my 4th birthday. Seeing my amended birth certificate as an adopted teen made me realize the entities involved in the adoption industry–state governments, adoption agencies–didn't think I was worth enough as a person to know my own truth or that my family wasn't good enough to warrant living honestly. And the 15-year-old me wondered if they were right. Perhaps I had to pretend because there was something inherently wrong with who I really was.

I'm well into adulthood now. I am married and the mother of two children. I have a successful career. I am reunited with both sides of my natural families. Yet, I am still stuck in that childish game of Let's Pretend. Because my legal birth certificate, the only one I'm allowed to use, still states that I am the biological child of two people who had nothing to do with my creation or birth.

I am legally still considered a child, unworthy of knowing my true self.

# Lee Herrick

## SALVATION

The blues is what mothers do
not tell their sons, in church
or otherwise, how their bodies
forgave them when their spirits
gave in, how you salvage love
by praying for something
acoustic, something clean
and simple like the ideal room,
one with a shelf with your three
favorite books and a photo
from your childhood, the one
of you with the big grin
before you knew about the blues.

I wonder what songs
my birth mother sang
in the five months she fed me
before she left me on the steps

of a church in South Korea.
I wonder if they sounded
like Sarah Chang's quivering bow,
that deep chant of a mother
saying goodbye to her son.
Who can really say?
Sometimes all we have is
the blues. The blues means
finding a song
in the abandonment, one

you can sing in the middle
of the night when you
remember that your Korean name,
Lee Kwang Soo, means bright
light, something that can illuminate
or shine, like tears,
little drops of liquefied God,

glistening down your brown face.
I wonder what songs my birth
mother sings and if she sings
them for me, what stories
her body might tell.
I have come to believe that
the blues is the body's salvation,
a chorus of scars to remind you
that you are here,

not where you feared you would be,

but here, flawed, angelic,

and full of light. I believe that

the blues is the spirit's wreckage,

examined and damaged but whole

again, more full and prepared than

it's ever been, quiet and still,

just as it was always meant to be.

# Matthew Salesses

## THE POWERS THAT BEAST

### The Voice We're Given

ADOPTEES SIT AT THE BOTTOM of the adoption power rankings. Maybe initially it's economics, the adoptee purchased by the adoptive parents; or the players' ages at the time of that transaction; or the historical context, that, at least transnationally, adoption is young and most adoptees are young. But the lingering truth is that adoptees remain subject to that power structure far into adulthood. The structure persists in how their (our) voice is valued. The adoptee voice seems always to be positioned either in contrast to or in agreement with the adoptive parent's (or agency's) voice—that is, perpetually in reference to those in power. It is an oft-overlooked danger of the Perpetual Child problem: the pretense of valuing the adoptee perspective while determining that value according to a *dis*empowering context.

Let's think of this in another way: a rhetoric scholar I know said recently that she didn't like her African American literature course because it used different terms for things she knew by other names in other courses. She wanted everyone to use the same terms, to make it easier on her (as, it must be said, a white student). She mentioned that this was the only time she was ever going to take an African American literature course, because it didn't intersect with her studies (of course), implying that the theories would be more relevant if they were part of the majority discussion. To his credit, the professor of record was quick to point out that African American literary scholars needed to create their own terms, at least at first, in order to break free from being seen only in relation to the majority, and from using terms that already belonged to someone else.

Or let's get away from academia, and think about how this applies to real life.

## The Voice We Give Ourselves

I would argue that the adoptee, or at least the transracial adoptee, is often bullied by other children as much for his similarities, or for daring to think there might be similarities, as for his differences. Probably he doesn't even realize this. The adopted child is often feared, often becomes a sort of reflection of insecurities. The adoptee often becomes Jung's Beast—the Other who needs to be accepted by the (accepted) Beauty in order for his own beauty to exist.

When I was growing up in my white town in Connecticut, I was so focused on my own fears that I barely recognized the fears other people had of me. Maybe this was why I bought into one of the great lies of bullying, that it was *I* who caused the teasing and insults and fights—that something wrong with *me*, not something wrong with how people *saw* me, was the reason I was singled out. If someone fought with me, the other person might change but I remained the common variable. I was just as ready as anyone to hate the side of me that wasn't the white kid I wished so badly to project (and be)—so badly I even denied to myself that I was not him. And this isn't to say I was an entirely unpopular kid; I was somewhere in the middle. I had my friends, but with those friends I didn't always feel entirely comfortable. One of the differences was that I seemed to have enemies no one else in my friend group had. I was in the middle, but to some, because I was adopted, or because I wasn't white, I would always be at the bottom.

I remember I had a friend who would constantly pick fights with me—I didn't know why. We would end up trying to get each other in a headlock at someone's birthday party, and then would laugh it off as having fun. I wasn't having fun. I don't think he was, either, but whenever I tried to avoid him I found him pushing at my wounds even more. When he fought with me, he got attention. He knew enough about me, as my supposed friend, to know exactly how to hurt me. I don't think I knew as much about myself in many ways. Sometimes it is the people who most want to hurt you who dig the fastest and deepest to your buried truths.

This friend had a shrink for a father and the daddy issues that perhaps went along with that. He was often shooting things with his BB gun or otherwise going through a prolonged stage of torturing animals. These were things about him we thought were cool: his interesting father, his violent urges. I can see now how insecure he was, but at the time the mask with which he covered that insecurity seemed enviable. Masks often do. Or they do for me. Maybe some part of me was impressed by the way he could be someone else on the outside.

Once, we got into a wrestling match at another friend's house—I was in high school by then, I think, and still having these fights—and I felt my anger come on more strongly than it ever had in previous encounters and with a determination I only had when I felt most wronged and justified, when I finally realized something was not my fault. Usually, I was happy to slip away as soon as possible, but this time, I tried harder and harder to hurt him. I wanted to do some lasting physical damage, to do something that would put an end to what I must have understood eventually, or on some level, as torment. In fact, I would dream of this friend doing crueler and crueler things to me—the scenarios we played out in real life were also stuck in my subconscious. This time, this fight, I threw elbows and tried to lock his arms and legs and get my arm around his throat. I got angry on the level of desperation, as if this was some last chance I had. I had to show him that he couldn't do this to me. And though I wasn't able to do any real damage (he was always stronger than me, or more aggressive with his strength, or more efficient with it, which he knew, of course), I think that for the first time, I scared him a little. I could feel that he was struggling, and that I might have eventually gotten the upper hand, when he broke away.

What he said then, though, is what I remember most well, and my answer to him is what really continues to torment me. He complimented me, as if this was all a game to him and he was happy to see me rise to the challenge, or as if he was some Mr. Miyagi and I was his pupil finally earning his respect. And in one of my worst moments, I felt proud of myself for that compliment. I *felt* respected by him. I felt my utter inferiority and a ridiculous pride that I had even come close to him.

It's difficult to write about how much I looked down on myself.

This wasn't even the friend who hurt me the worst for my seeming inferiority, not the one who turned his back on our friendship and pretended it had never existed as he climbed the popularity ranks, or the friend with whom I thought I was extremely close but who I have realized over many years never believed the same. This friend, the BB gun friend, was a friend who seemed the entire time to believe that we were friends and that this was our (natural) dynamic.

Now, maybe obviously, we are not friends anymore. I'm sure he has realized that we were never friends. We were afraid of each other. It wasn't just me, I see now. Or we had recognized in each other something about ourselves that we were afraid of. If I look at the parts of myself I'd rather not see, even now, I think I must have located in him a boy whose father could have understood him if he had only let him. I think he recognized in me a boy who had his same violent urges, that same deep-seeded rage, under the mask I was trying so hard to wear. Maybe he was trying to draw me out as a way of drawing himself out.

Or maybe I really was the only one with the issues. How can one ever be sure?

This friend eventually made a point of not inviting me to his wedding, though we were still supposedly on good terms then. I didn't invite him to mine, though I didn't invite most of my friends from childhood. I was still not over the way I saw *myself* in my relationships with them. I'm still not over that.

I don't know what I would do if I saw this friend now. I hate being reminded of that time. I hate that I will still regress to who they thought I was, to the dynamics we had then. I hate that they can define me in their ways, without my having any input, from something they must see as inherent. I will probably never go to a high school reunion. I have only one good friend remaining from high school, and whenever she suggests we try to have a little get-together with other classmates, she seems to know ahead of time that I will turn her down. I know that to be around those classmates, I will feel as if I never grew up.

## The Voice We Take

The power structure with that friend, where I only felt

85

on even ground, and where I congratulated myself for reaching that even ground, when he finally acknowledged me—I see this same power structure (this same *beast*ing) played out in many adoption essays I read online.

Even in the current adoption climate, the adoptee is caught between, spoken for, treated as a purpose, or a context, as a way to improve the adoptive parent or agency, as something to be learned from or ignored, as less an individual with her own agency and more a contribution to the agency of someone else. Of course children may start out being (and providing) a purpose, in some ways. Adults decide to have children (sometimes). Adults decide to give children up (sometimes). Adults decide to adopt. But valuing adoptees means actually valuing adoptees' voices, letting them talk for themselves and not interpreting what they say for one's own purpose. It's like this: sometimes I read these articles by adoptive parents talking about their kids as blessings, as gifts, and saying what they have done for their kids, taking them back to their homeland and how good that's been for them, for the kids and for themselves. So often, this is all second hand, all the parent's account. Sometimes the parent talks about what she has learned about her child's original culture, how having an adopted child has opened *her* eyes to Asia or so forth. It's unbearably parent-centric—all aimed at what the parent can (or rather, *has*) learned. And when an article is actually about the adoptee and yet written as if the adoptive parent *knows* what is going on in the adoptee's head, how do I believe that? How does that parent believe that? I can write an entire book about denial, and even if I knew exactly how I felt, I would not have wanted to make my parents pity me, or feel confused about me, or, worse, try to explain or to fix me. I suspect it's like that for others, though of course I am loathe to do what I am arguing against: to put words in other adoptees' mouths, no matter how I think I understand. My point is that the adoptive parent is not the one who should be judging whether the adoptee really understands or does not, is happy or is not, is adjusting or is not, is Beauty or is Beast.

It is a problem of its own that adoptees ourselves have trouble telling how we really feel. But how complicated that becomes when held up to the standard and scrutiny of the adoption power structure.

I was at a talk recently on education, where the speaker was discussing how people had been wrong to think an early education program had failed—at the time they hadn't been able to study the long long-term results. They were measuring the results via testing. In the short-term, the tests seemed promising, and in the medium-term, the tests seemed to show nothing, or only temporary improvements, so researchers had thought the program was a failure. Yet years later, studying those children, it seems that early education had extremely deep-seeded effects, resulting in children being less likely to do something that ended them up in jail, less likely to become pregnant at a young age, and so on. Even when the test scores seemed to show that the effect of early schooling went away by the time they were teens. The education system wasn't an effective way of measuring the education system.

Maybe it is a matter of what we are subject to. For it is not that I think these adoption articles, these evaluations, these studies, are a problem of empathy. I'm not saying adoptive parents are wrong to think about how their kids feel, or even to imagine those feelings. I believe these parents when they say they love and cherish their children. I believe they are trying and I can believe that they are trying to see things from the adoptee perspective. I believe they talk to their kids, that their kids say what appears in the articles. I even believe that writing about their kids could be helpful to empathy, could help them understand their sons and daughters through the mere act of trying to put themselves in those shoes. The problem is, it reinforces the idea that the adoptive parent has the authority over the adoptee, and even the adoptee's feelings and thoughts and growth. It reinforces the idea that the adoptive parent is the one who tells the adoptee's story.

What makes me saddest, though, is when I read adoptee essays in which the writers seem to assert the same. When they have to explain themselves in comparison or contrast to the adoptive parent. I have been there. Often this stance is by necessity, is important in thinking about one's audience. Often the adoptee writer has to write an entire essay of, "That's not how it is," or even, "Don't speak for us." I may have even done so here. It takes so much space before the essay can make its own territory, until the adoptee writer can escape the (e)valuation of the power structure and wonder for herself. That is where the adoptee has a power and a context of her own, where she can say, this is a question outside of any (granted) authority. This is a question I am asking myself, not for you to legitimize or strike down or make real, but because I have to ask it and it is mine to ask. And if I am asking it also for you, then consider what I don't know on my terms, not as a plea for help or acceptance.

The adoptee voice matters because the adoptee says so.

# Jennifer Bao Yu "Precious Jade" Jue-Steuck

---

SWINGING THE BALANCE OF THE UNIVERSE: MEMORIES, MANTRAS & MUSINGS ON THE MIXED-BLESSINGS OF THE ICONIC MYTH OF 'THE PERPETUAL CHILD' IN ADOPTION

**"One child...can swing the balance of the universe."**

—Madeleine L'Engle

*This piece was inspired by Mary Child and Mary D. Healy, and is dedicated in loving memory of cousin Danielle Mai Ting Jue (1982-2001)—who taught me how to pay attention—and grandmother ("Popo") Lucy Jue (1911-1995), an orphaned girl from Los Angeles who showed me the beauty and colors of my 'wings,' and introduced me to her shimmering 1930s Shanghai, the place she once called home.*

# PART I: MEMORIES

When I was a young girl I built a graveyard. It sat at the entrance of our lakeside summer property at Branch Pond Lake in Maine (about a half an hour from Acadia National Park), where I spent nearly every childhood summer with my family from ages 2 to 15. I created this cemetery when I was 8, and expanded and tended to it each summer like a dedicated gardener. At the time, I didn't know why I felt a need to build a graveyard. My Mom encouraged its creation (she was an English major, and liked the fact that my graveyard had a literary theme); my Dad clearly thought the whole thing to be a bit odd (how many 8-year-olds are obsessed with building cemeteries?).

I was a voracious reader from a young age, so the thematic aspect of my graveyard had one special rule: only characters (from novels) who truly loved one another, but for various reasons were separated, could hold a gravestone in the cemetery. The gravestones were large granite rocks I found in the woods surrounding the lake. I painted their names on the rocks, with each gravestone dedicated in loving memory of two separated individuals. Mine was the Père Lachaise of characters (which included some historical figures), mostly from novels: Romeo & Juliet, Jane Eyre & Mr. Rochester, Lady Jane Grey (famous for being Queen of England for nine days, before being beheaded by her cousin, Mary Queen of Scots) & Lady Jane Grey's husband (also beheaded). By the time I was eleven, Catherine & Heathcliff were added (separated in the moors of West Yorkshire in *Wuthering Heights* due to Cathy's death), along with several other characters from the Western literary canon.

In addition to a single gravestone for each couple, symbolically reuniting the separated, each pair were given an elaborate ceremony by the lake, complete with a bouquet of wild flowers from the woods, their own floating boat with their names and information about them and why, I thought, we should remember them. I then blessed each couple and released them to be embraced by the rippling waters of the beautiful lake.

Each summer my graveyard grew as I read more and more novels, and learned of more and more separations of "family members" and loved ones in fiction. My graveyard was the first and last place I greeted in Maine each summer, until I was nearly grown and left for university to study literature and creative writing at New York University's Tisch School of the Arts.

At the time, I didn't realize what I do know now: my graveyard—one for mostly fictional characters—was the safest way that I could express grief about being separated from my birthfamily and, in particular, from my birthmother. By creating a graveyard for mostly 'fictional characters' who were separated, I could safely express my own grief of separation from my genetic family and ancestors. By building a permanent graveyard at our beloved summer property in Maine, I could grieve annually at our summertime 'ancestral home' in the woods, and make my own child ceremonies, important rituals for remembrance and loss.

What I didn't realize growing up is that I had experienced a real loss: a Motherloss and a birthfamily loss, which effectively meant the loss and social erasure of my entire genetic family. I knew that I had technically been separated from my birthfamily (or no longer lived with them), but I wasn't taught that it was a legitimate loss since they were still living when I was adopted (and therefore had not 'passed away'), as legitimate as that of any other child or adult losing their mother. It seemed that though I was separated, I had been offered fantastic, beyond-wildest-imagination substitute parents, so somehow the fact that my entire genetic family went 'missing' seemed to be negated, cancelled or rubbed out. Most noticeably, no one seemed to mourn with me. No one even seemed to think that I might be mourning at all. So I mourned alone. In secret (and at the time, mostly unconsciously), through child games and 'play ceremonies' for the dead or separated fictional characters in the classical Western cannon.

I separated my loss, severed from my realm of consciousness, into 'Fictions' and 'Facts.' My 'Facts' included my Present, my adoptive family. My 'Fictions' included my Past, my genetic family. By the time I went away to college in New York City, I had 'rehearsed' my origin story so well, repeatedly sorting piles of information into 'Facts' and 'Fictions,' that I no longer knew what was real and what was imaginary. My story—effectively the story told to me by my parents and extended (adoptive) family and community—was slowly digested, uncontested, fossilized into 'Fact,' 'real life' and rote memory.

It was only when my (adoptive) mother passed away from cancer that this original and primal first Motherloss erupted, seemingly 'from out of the blue.' As I found myself mourning my adoptive mother, I simultaneously experienced parallel and acute feelings of loss for my birthmother, strangely merging my until-then-clearly-distinguishable lifetime piles of 'Facts' and 'Fictions.'

This double process seemed strange and bewildering, because I had (for most of my life) never been consciously aware that I had even "lost" a mother. As I examined the bones of my life—a socially dead mother (biological) and a physically dead mother (adoptive)—many thoughts emerged. I had a mother, so how could I have lost her? Further, my birthmother was still well and alive when I was adopted, so there was no 'loss' of life, no death that I ought to be mourning. My birthmother seemed as real as fantasy, as fictitious as Jane Eyre or Romeo's Juliet. Most of all, how could I mourn her if I could not remember her? And yet, my mourning process for Birthmother was as real—neither fake nor fictitious—as it was for my 'real (adoptive) mother's' passing from ovarian cancer. What's more, as I traveled down the voyage of the bereaved, I realized, slowly and steadily over the course of many years, that I had been mourning my birthmother for my entire life; but it was so privately and quietly hidden in the secret subterranean closet of my subconscious—having been forced underground—that even I had forgotten its once-upon-a-time perennial presence.

This unraveling of mourning felt like the peeling off of a never-ending, regenerative snake's skin—as the labyrinth of my bereavement for my mother progressed year after year, anniversary after anniversary of her death—my bereavement for my birthmother also slowly emerged with its own limbs, body, spirit, a phantom presence with a heartbeat as loud and clear as my own...

## PART II: MUSINGS ON A 'PERPETUAL CHILD'

The body hungers for food; the spirit hungers to *be known*, to shimmer in blissful connection, to receive the sustenance of the spectral, and to sink into the soft sensation of being blanketed by a divine embrace of love, understanding and peaceful acceptance.

Sadly, many of us live on war-time rations of love. The love that we so desperately need and crave may seem beyond reach. Real connection? The truth is that many of us feel more connected to our pets than we do to our so-called human family members. Is it any wonder that there is a serious shortage of soulful love vibrations, and a gross over-distribution of bodily weight in our country? We may be rich in dollars, or pounds or yen, but poor in a currency not currently traded on any stock market: the currency of true connection, the kind that invites our spirits to dance and dip in and out of the constellation of matter that connects everything from our tiny bodily cells to the stardust in the universe.

Do you feel truly connected and seen, in a spiritual sense, by others? The myth of the perpetual child renders many adopted people 'invisible' in the realm of the everyday world. Maybe if I could *see* you, if you could see me, if I could reach out and touch you in that most authentic place filled with incandescent radiance, maybe you would feel like you could truly emerge in your divine human form, as you were meant to be...as you were born to be. Maybe, just maybe, by really *seeing* one another, we ground and root each other in our spiritual forms energetically vibrating in our human manifestations. Maybe part of the myth of the perpetual child is simply a manifestation of our inability to really and truly see, to deeply listen and to understand.

Perhaps you could try the following experiment? For 30 days, I would like to offer you unconditional love, support and encouragement. I offer this to myself and to everyone I come into contact with. I want—for 30 days—for you to live as if no one has ever hurt you. Maybe by recognizing, honoring, processing and claiming our human disconnections, we can actually *be* in real connection. Let's be energetically free and joyful. Let's be so alive that we become bigger than our pain. Maybe when we feel a loss (loss of authentic connection, loss of visibility, loss of place, loss of origin), what we really need to do is simply give from the heart, offer a sense of peace and connection and wholeness and search for the beauty in everything around us. What's a perpetual child? A myth. A story. You, dear reader, are real. You are divine. You transcend names, titles, assumptions. I want to see you energetically alive. I want to hear your voices. I want to remember your stories and write them in the sky, vibrating with the heart of the universe.

If you courageously shifted your own awareness and attitude right now, how might your life transcend the human shadow into new forms of pure light, love and radiance? How might your inner child be both 'perpetual' and perennial? Could we turn the myth inside out, shake it upside down, and see what YOU drops out?

## PART III: MANTRAS FOR A GLOBAL GENERATION

*This section is dedicated to YOU,*
*and to my younger sisters of the heart around the world,*
*who each have unique gifts to share*
*and are already adding to the annals of*
*adoption and women's history.*

Alana Mouchard, Bo Allen, Emi Yamada-Heidner, Erin Dickenson, Jasmine Pyne, Juleigh Duke, Katie Lynne Cohen, Kim Prusak, Li Catzel, Lily Peachment, Ly Hoang, Lynne de Zagon, Lu Ann Connor, Maeve Murphy, Mallory McFarland, Mia Yamada-Heidner, Phoebe Peachment, Rachel Keller, Róisín Murphy, Sabrina Orlins, Sonny Allen and all the G2 girls around the world who have given so much to create a global 'Network of Care' for future generations.

*Dear Sisters of the Heart,*
*Thank you for being Glorious,*
*and for inspiring me to do my best in the face of all odds.*
*You are always a part of my family,*
*and I love you all very much.*

———◦✕◦———

My Mom nods, looking down from Heaven, relief flooding her face. Her voice travels across ghostly lands and ghostly galaxies and seven high seas, soaring over tall mountains that tickle the blue belly of the sky with their rounded tips.

I forgot to give you this, she whispers. I come from ghostly lands to bring you this gift—the gift of my living words. It may come in memories of dreams of sleepless nights and salty tears, but in it lies all of my hopes that you will write every day of your life as your truest self. You are capable of things that I could only dream of, because you are overcoming challenges that I could not. Inside of you is not just my courage and strength, but also an alchemy of authenticity and ability from your birthmother, and from her mother and from me, from my mother, and from all our great grandmothers before us, an endless cord eons long...awaiting the start of a ritual—that ritual is the gift of you. With every breath you take, our collective hope herein lies. You are authentic, powerful, lovable, beautiful, kind, worthy, creative, and capable. Both of our families—by birth and by love—are so proud of you. Go forth with these gifts, removed from our wombs by distance—and by hope—but connected by our words, our breath stitched onto this very sheet of paper by ink, sewed to an invisible live cord eons long, by the geometry of our greatest gifts, our collective sorrows, and the mystical mana of our mothers' enduring love. Remember—

> We stand
> all of us drawn here
> by an invisible cord eons long
> awaiting the start of a ritual
> removed from its womb
> by distance and by hope...*

This ritual is the Gift of You.

May all who read this sacred social contract of the spirit, body and heart, hereby stand witness, attest and know forever more that...

I am a world citizen of a wondrous universe, and a contributing member of a global generation. I am filled with wisdom, serenity, light, wild ecstasy, creativity, passion, love, divine integrity and possibility. I defy limiting definitions and explore the mixed-blessings of modern life, including the absent and present pieces of my motherline threads, of my fatherline threads, and of my many mixed, evolving identities—past, present and future. I love to travel (metaphorically /—physically), keep it simple, and follow my dreams. I share my unique resources to give something back, and in doing so, I bless others, myself, my blood and adoptive families, and the world, in which I fully belong at all times—spiritually, emotionally, physically, and historically. I fully accept myself in profound love and gratitude of our ever-lasting connection to our spiritual guides, our planet and our celestial stars.

---

Let it be known that I have the divine right to be here, in this place at this time, that I am—following the footsteps of Jennifer Arndt-Johns—a 'citizen of the world' and part of a global generation.

Let it be known that I have the right to have my voice heard, with respect and dignity.

Let it be known that I have the right to my histories— all of them.

Let it be known that I have the right to express sadness, frustration, anger, joy and love for my history and all of its missing-present-absent pieces.

Let it be known that I have the right to remember and to honor my blood family with love, dignity, hope, respect and gratitude for giving me life and the ability to express myself.

Let it be known that I have the right to be authentic,

both with myself and with others.

Let it be known that I have the right to be appreciated for who I really am, including my dreams and hopes, past-lives and future-lives, and for this moment in the eternal present of our planet, when my own 'inner child' may be "swinging the balance of the universe" in mysterious, mystical ways.

Let it be known that we all have the right to be loved unconditionally, no matter where we came from, or how we entered our beautiful universe.

———————————

*This passage is an excerpt from "Poon," a poem by my mother Janet Jue (1941-1999), published in Sowing Ti Leaves: Writings by Multicultural Women, edited by Sarie Sachie Hylkema and Dr. Mitsuye Yamada, 2nd edition (Irvine, California: MCWW Press, 1990). "Part III: Mantras for a Global Generation" includes an excerpt from my article "Goodnight Moon, Goodnight Mom," published in the anthology From Home to Homeland: What Adoptive Families Need to Know Before Making a Return Trip to China, edited by Debra Jacobs, Iris Chin Ponte, and Leslie Kim Wang (St. Paul, Minnesota: Yeong & Yeong Press, 2010).

# Mei-Mei Akwai Ellerman

## Coming Full Circle

*When I was One,*
*I had just begun.*
*When I was Two,*
*I was nearly new.*
*When I was Three,*
*I was hardly me.*
*When I was Four,*
*I was not much more.*
*When I was Five, I was just alive.*
*But now I am Six, I'm as clever as clever,*
*So I think I'll be six now for ever and ever.*

A.A. Milne, *Now We are Six,* 1927

ONE OF MY FAVORITE POEMS as a child. A poem I knew by heart and would chant in a sing-song voice over and over, beguiled by the rhythm, the simple images that appealed to me as a six-year-old, all eyes and ears, yet becoming conscious of my own sense of self, my identity. "When I was One, I had just begun..." In retrospect, winsome as it may sound, it doesn't extend beyond the awareness of Christopher Robin, or any other child of the same age, caught up in the exuberance of sudden self-discovery. And no matter how enraptured we may be of a certain moment or period of our existence, yearning to capture it forever and seal it and ourselves in a luminous, womb-like bubble, time and our life-journey are destined to flow inexorably forward.

According to traditional Chinese calculations, an individual's beginning includes the ten lunar months of pregnancy, so when born, he or she is considered almost one. Continuously nurtured, while swimming, floating and somersaulting in the swirling waters of the maternal womb, at the end of the gestation period, a fully formed baby emerges into blinding light, assaulted by alien sounds, smells, and sensations. Deprived without warning of the protective warmth of his or her natural environment, the soothing swishing of the amniotic fluid and reassuring maternal heartbeat, the fetus, now a helpless yet independent being, experiences the first and most dramatic psychic and physical separation, marked by the sudden intake of life-giving air as the cord is cut, and a distinctive unforgettable cry. Normally the infant is placed directly on its mother's chest where it can once more hear the familiar cadence, though from the outside. Then, quickly bathed and swaddled, it is returned to enveloping arms that cradle and offer a new haven, while it instinctively nuzzles, in search of the source of nourishment that will sustain and ensure growth and development for months to come.

For an adoptee, that special, immediate reconnection after struggling to emerge into an foreign world, is either short-lived or never takes place. Though there are claims that some babies may retain implicit memories from a very early stage, I personally have no recollection of leaving my natural mother's womb, of the first ten days passed in a private hospital in New York City, cared for by nurses and staff, and sadly, not even the faintest memory of the seven months spent under the ministrations of my Italian foster mother. On the other hand, I can almost recreate in my mind's eye the heartwarming reception that greeted my arrival at Whately Glen, my parents' property in Western Massachusetts, purchased in the early '40s. The story of my adoption was among my most cherished bedtime tales.

My mother, Elsa Dagmar Oiesen, born in Wonsan, Korea in 1900, explained that I had come into her life at 8 months, long before I could grasp the implications of what it meant to be adopted. Youngest daughter of her Danish father, James Frederick Oiesen [1857-1928] and her Chinese mother, Akwai Yang [1866-1942], my mother left China just after turning 11 to join her four older siblings in the United States. Her father served as Commissioner of the Chinese Imperial Maritime Customs in China and Korea for over 40 years, became British Consul of the Land of the Morning Sun in the late 1800's and Danish Minister to China in 1921. Her Chinese mother, defying traditions observed unopposed for centuries, was disowned, disinherited and ostracized by her wealthy family when, in 1885, at age 19, she chose to follow my grandfather, the "tall, blond, blue-eyed devil." For both educational reasons and predictable issues of racial discrimination, especially in the early 1900's, all five children were sent abroad, to private schools in New England and placed under the tutelage of guardians.

James Oiesen visited his young every five years, when granted furlough. Their mother would reunite with her adult children in 1927, and due to tragic circumstances, only for a mere two years. In 1929 she returned to China with one of the seven daughters she had adopted after her biological children left for the West-one for each child to whom she had given birth, including twins who died at birth. My mother and her siblings thus grew up deprived of regular contact with the parents whom they all adored. The flow of letters, hundreds of letters, exchange of presents and the periodic yearlong visits by their papa, kept the family bonds and love alive. Yet photos of the children, especially when young, taken soon after their arrival from Asia, reveal more than a hint of melancholy mixed with touching stoicism as they gazed into the camera's lens.

Adoption was a time-honored tradition in China in the late 1800's and early 1900's, both from within the extended family and as a means to offer education and better prospects to children born into less fortunate circumstances. My grandmother hired private tutors, extended the same privileges and imparted as loving yet strict an upbringing to her seven adopted daughters as she would have given her children, if not separated by the vast expanse of the Pacific Ocean. The longing on behalf of all family members to be reunited transpires throughout the rich correspondence I was fortunate enough to inherit. The reasons for the separation were complex and would require too lengthy an explanation.

At 21, in her final semester at Ann Arbor, my mother contracted tuberculosis of the peritoneum. The physicians at Mass General did their utmost to save her, [seven years before Alexander Fleming discovered penicillin], but could offer no cure other than complete rest and pure mountain air. Mother sacrificed four years of her youth to what would be a complete recovery, save that she was left unable to bear children. Though courted by many, including a Danish prince, in 1936 she married my father, Lewis Dennison Bement, son of the founder of the Bement School in Deerfield, MA, and six years her junior. Handsome, the life of any party, the king of the cornet, Daddy was indubitably charismatic but equally irresponsible when it came to women and alcohol.

When WWII broke out in 1939, my mother took in my "siblings", Binkie, Peter and Gina, three British children, for a period of over five years. Entrusted to her care by their parents who were close friends, she ensured that the

14-, 6-, and 4-year olds were spared the trauma of daily air raids, bombings and a potential German invasion. When returned to their respective families, they all experienced severe issues as they missed my mother's full hearted love and exceptional approach to child rearing. I have remained close to all three throughout the years. Sadly, just weeks ago, I learned that Binkie had passed away at the age of 86. We always felt like real sisters and she emphatically stated that she was far closer to my mother than to her own.

In 1943, Mother and Daddy learned that a Chinese baby, born at an exclusive NYC clinic, was awaiting a family. One of the two parents had to be Chinese, strongly attached to his or her cultural heritage, highly educated and of a certain milieu. I can still hear my mother's mellifluous voice recounting my special story:

> *Dorothy Woodford, a social worker and an old friend, discovered you one day while visiting a private hospital in Manhattan. When she saw you through the nursery, her thoughts flew to Daddy and me; "I have found the most enchanting baby for you!" She described you from top to toe. Elated, I hopped into my car and headed for New York. The second I lay eyes on you, my heart melted.*

> *Daddy and I filled out stacks of forms. The staff at the adoption agency interviewed us, checked and rechecked our backgrounds. You were a very important little person. Instead of the anticipated yearlong wait, the Agency determined we met all the adoption conditions: we were worthy of you. Just months from the time I first saw you, you were ours!*

Before signing the final papers, my parents were informed that my natural mother had died in childbirth; there was no mention of my father.

From the very first day, I was surrounded by love, the center of a large, vibrant, diverse family, which included the children at my grandmother's school, 10 English Setters and a Scottish terrier, my self-appointed guardian. My childhood unfolded as a continuous adventure: almost a year in Denmark when I turned 4, followed by a six-month-long stay in Mexico, then back to the United States. When Mother finally reached the excruciating decision to divorce my father, a businessman and an amazing jazz musician, my life took yet another turn. Daddy played with all the greats-Louis Armstrong, Benny Goodman, the Dorsey Brothers, Gerry Mulligan, Dave Brubeck, but as many of his generation, he fell victim to the bottle, in his case, bourbon. Though he clearly loved me, one day he disappeared and only visited sporadically, always witty, debonair, but a fleeting presence. Even in the rare dreams I have had of him over my lifetime, he always vanishes after a warm, light-hearted encounter.

In 1951, at the age of 9, my mother and I moved to the South of France. In part due to several unpleasant episodes of racial discrimination I had experienced at school, in part because Mother felt the need to map out new space for herself and was a firm believer in the European educational system and known tolerance of diversity. I attended the local village school of L'Isle -sur -La Sorgue. Lacking even rudimentary language skills, I moved from first to third grade in a single academic year and ended up speaking flawless French. The second month I experienced firsthand the malice of discrimination-not against myself [I easily integrated], but against three "gypsy" children whose colorful caravans were lined up in a circle on the outskirts of the village. All older [due to continuous interruption in their schooling], their hair unkempt, dressed in tattered, outgrown clothes, they were placed at the very back of the classroom, their benches against the wall, a considerable distance from the last row. All the children shunned them during recess. I tried to befriend them as I sensed that they felt "other" yet even my being different was insufficient to penetrate the barriers they had erected from a very young age.

The following fall found us in Italy, first in Alassio on the Ligurian Coast, at the time a sleepy fishing village where we resided for five years, then on to the Florence, city of art, music, history and inestimable cultural riches. Italy became my true home for a full eleven years. Not surprisingly, given the times, I was always the only Asian in these different settings, not to mention the only adopted child, but neither raised any issues. At times my mother would teasingly comment that I exhibited more Italian traits, being so emotionally open, dramatic, operatic, than either American or Chinese.

Changing schools (ten times in all, not counting colleges), languages and cultures were both a challenge and source of understandable apprehension. Even when younger, it was easy to adapt. Outwardly a gregarious, spirited, rambunctious child, I made friends with ease and always fitted in, one of the attributes passed on by my mother who had taken her cosmopolitan father's words to heart, "Wherever you hang your hat, is home."

Adopted children tend to acclimate to most circumstances, to genuinely blend in, to be chameleons, as my mother was, in fact. The opposite also occurs, alas, far too often: if a true bond fails to develop with their new family or they are bullied at school or feel excluded, a frequent occurrence, children can go through periods of profound rebellion, anger, total lack of self-esteem, or turn inwards, become loners convinced that nobody truly understands. Some are unable to shed these weighty chains, even as adults. In fact, scarred for life, they take up the banner of rage and injustice to proclaim that they were treated as simple objects in a monetary transaction. Today, in our global economy and the dark under belly of the internet, tens and tens of thousands of children become trafficking victims, some destined to be sold off to unscrupulous Adoption Agencies, others doomed to even more horrifying fates, consigned to the thriving sex industry.

The need to achieve, to shine and prove oneself, seems a drive present in a majority of adoptees and persists into adulthood. A preeminent and unique example is Steve Jobs. I always felt my drive stemmed from my accomplished mother, but looking back, I sense that at an unconscious level, "succeeding" in my case neither expected or required, was also a means of making oneself worthy, worthy of the steadfast love, of maintaining the safe harbor, as well as giving back the gift of having been chosen.

Throughout my childhood, life was colorful, exciting, a continuous adventure, with Mother always at my side, my constant point of reference, defender and supporter. I never gave a second thought to the fact she hadn't given birth to me. As I grew older and other children would spontaneously comment that we didn't look alike [my mother, though half Chinese, had inherited her father's Scandinavian build and complexion-only a faint hint of her Asian lineage showed in the subtle slant of her eyes], I would proudly announce that I was adopted. End of discussion.

Mother reached out to anyone in need of comfort, a shoulder to cry on, an empathetic listener. She was the epitome of the maternal figure, the nurturer and consoler. Even as a child I must have instinctively followed her example. When I was 15, I remember wanting us to adopt a 9-year-old Italian boy who resided in a nearby Catholic orphanage. At the time, we lived on the outskirts of Florence. His name was Antonio. I recall his long mesh of brown hair that partially obscured his freckled face, his pale demeanor and liquid brown eyes. It broke my heart when he would whisper, "Why can't I live with your family all the time?"

As the years went by, even in adolescence, I was drawn to classmates who were especially sensitive and going through the typical *Sturm und Drang* that roils the soul, often leaving one crushed, only to quickly rally for the next oncoming storm. We immersed ourselves in Thomas Mann, Dostoevsky, Proust, Camus and Sartre, searching, searching for answers to existential questions and inner torment. Was I angrier than others? Did I rebel? Did I wish to cling to the golden experiences of my early childhood rather than face the hard choices, the complexity of forming and dismantling relationships, moving out of my comfort zone? Hardly. I always looked forward with anticipation to the next hurdle to conquer, even within myself. My sense of identity remained strong throughout. I was my mother's daughter who felt as protective of her [thus less likely to act out, though I did have my moments] as she did of me-she never turned out her light until I was safely home, even if it was 3:00 in the morning. An ingenious way of keeping me on track.

Protectiveness in adoptees, even at an early age, is instinctive. I knew that Mother had suffered a great deal due to the divorce [although she never shared any details]. I took pains to spare her anxiety and possible additional hurt even though she presented such a strong façade. She believed in me unconditionally. When I first fell in love at 16, it threw me into turmoil, not wanting to go against my Mother's value system, but choosing to act spontaneously. Keeping secrets, feeling profoundly guilty, were a source of true anguish. Of course I later discovered that Mother had guessed all along... Both then, as in the future, she gave me the freedom to choose, to make my own mistakes and learn from them, continuing to guide me from the sidelines. Her greatest gift of all, was that when the appropriate time arrived, she "let me go," allowed me to live my own life, always supportive even when she disagreed.

Our home in Florence teemed with girls, approximately my own age, whose parents sent them abroad to broaden their perspectives and acquire a new language. Mother didn't wish me to grow up as a single child. She and my courtesy aunt, her business partner, also ran a summer camp in Vermont for five years, dedicated exclusively to drama [Shakespeare], and the arts [painting, music, sculpture, dance]. So, in a sense I had numerous siblings, year round, though ever changing. Several of them remain my closest friends to this day. Kinship can cover such a wide range of relationships.

My conflicts, when they emerged in adolescence focused far more on my parents' divorce than on being adopted, the unjustifiable pain Daddy had inflicted on my mother who outwardly maintained her dignity and poise while suffering from intense migraines, insomnia and ulcers of the mouth. I turned against jazz, all the rage among my peers, and in a country where drinking three to four glasses of wine at a meal is taken as a matter of course, fumed over my boyfriend's consumption of a single serving of vino rosso.

Not long after, my father died of cancer of the stomach. I hadn't seen him in several years. His slow and agonizing death as the cancer spread to other organs and to his skin, mitigated any negative feelings I had towards him. Mother, who had borne the brunt of his behavior, once again exemplified the grace and wisdom I would come to so appreciate and emulate years later when my own 25-year-long marriage came to an end. She spoke only of the happy times together, reminisced about his sense of humor, his charm, musical genius and doting ways as a father when present. "Life is too short to dwell on the negatives. Best to hold on to the good memories." [My former husband and I have remained close friends. Only reasonable since we met when we were 19].

For the first time, after Daddy's death, I began to muse about my natural father. I rarely dwelt on my mother, a shadowy figure I believed had slipped away in the effort to bring me into the world. Guilt-ridden, I unconsciously stifled any underlying emotions. Instead I envisioned my father's hand, setting down the rigid stipulations for my adoption, thus concerned about my future, yet not sufficiently engaged to keep me, or even search for me in later years. I felt torn between gratitude for ensuring that I was embraced by the most remarkable mother I could have imagined, yet resentful that he had walked away from me when I was a mere infant, defenseless, utterly vulnerable.

Deep down, at the core of my being, I recognize today that as the decades passed, even as I married, taught and nurtured hundreds of students over 30 years, gave birth to two unique, beautiful, accomplished children, [Derek and Mei-Ling, today ages 35 and 40, the first dedicated to human rights and creating global sustainable programs to rescue millions enslaved worldwide, the second to give voice to thousands of powerless Chinese women migrant domestic workers in Beijing], unofficially "adopted" or became a second mother to numerous other children, now adults with little ones of their own, deep down, buried and encased in layer upon layer of protective armor, there was a small unacknowledged void, yearning to be recognized and filled.

My mother was convinced she knew my natural father's identity, in part based on my adoption conditions. He obviously was an intellectual, cosmopolitan, from a certain milieu. She actually was well acquainted with him and his entire family during her years in Paris between 1934-38. She would often speak of him to reassure me that he was someone of whom I could be proud. I studiously read his vast output of literature, translations of Chinese classics, philosophical treatises, novels and endless essays. I stood in front of the hazy bathroom mirror in our Florentine home, comparing the photos on his book jackets with my own reflection. I detected a certain resemblance... In fact, Mother was mistaken, as I would find out years later. But even when hovering close to death, though I didn't realize her time was nigh, she affirmed once again, "I am sure ...was your father. He probably had a winter/spring relationship." She wanted me to feel complete.

The first Adoption conference I attended at MIT in the spring of 2011 with Jennifer Bao Yu Jue-Steuck, threw open the gates and ushered me into the adoption community, forcing me to take notice of voices that had been mere whispers within, barely audible. Listening to natural mothers speak of the life-long longing and pain they experienced from having surrendered their child, plunged me into a vortex of heretofore-unexplored emotions. My more than decade-long ongoing quests for both my Mother's family history, including the Danish, Korean, Thai, and Chinese connections, and for my natural Mother's identity, assumed new meaning and urgency. The stories of searches, some successful, other futile, of reunions, of the indescribable grief experienced on all sides, was shattering. Fortunately, other adoptees, natural parents and adoptive parents also shared happy outcomes, though rarely without conflicts.

Listening to the heartfelt tales, I finally admitted to myself that loss, abandonment and any form of perceived rejection, had impacted me in ways I had never acknowledged; that the inner child in me would always be vulnerable to them, even today as I enter my 70s. A challenge with which I still need to grapple, to heal and reassure that child that the adult me is a strong, confident and powerful protector, capable of facing any amount of pain, and successfully processing it.

My mother remained youthful for her age, both physically and mentally, well into her 80s. She continued to travel, venturing to exotic sites and revisiting old haunts, from the coastal villages of Northern Spain to the mosques and open markets of Istanbul; weaving in and out of the Norwegian Fjords by postal boat, and viewing the midnight sun at the Arctic Circle, not to mention yearly trips between Italy (where she had settled in 1952) and Massachusetts, where I lived with my family.

As she approached ninety, Mother developed increasingly acute health problems: severe osteoporosis, Meniere's syndrome, crippling arthritis that led to double hip replacement, and noticeable deafness, only somewhat alleviated by hearing aids. She, who in her youth had graced ballrooms across Europe and America, and even after her mid-eighties glided effortlessly from room to room in the Tuscan farmhouse where she retired, began to move at a slower and more deliberate pace. Within a year she graduated from one to two canes, and eventually to a walker.

Mother accepted without protest that her once lithe, athletic body was betraying her bit by bit. I, in contrast, reacted to the dramatic changes with mixed emotions, tenderness and protectiveness on the one hand, but uncharacteristic frustration on the other. Where was the mother I knew, the woman who had taken me into her life at the age of eight months, made me her very own, nurtured me and fought battles on my behalf until I was able to stand up for both myself and others? What had happened to the mother, who invariably had responded to my every need, from infancy to the heartache of my divorce in 1992, yet had inspired me to cultivate a strong spirit of independence and to become a mighty force in my own right. I was unsettled by my response to the predictable symptoms of aging that finally had caught up with my mother.

Upon reflection, I realized that my discomfort stemmed from a web of complex feelings: fear of losing the unwavering support I had counted upon from earliest childhood; denial or unwillingness to acknowledge that my mother was entering the final phase of her life, and exasperation at my powerlessness to stem the inevitable process. I was petrified that the advancing physical disabilities might herald even more profound, far-reaching changes. Above all I felt woefully unprepared to take on the foreseeable reversal of roles, to become my mother's mother.

I found myself going through a lengthy mourning process as Mother relinquished, one by one, the emblems of her autonomy. But as she came to accept an increasingly restricted range of activities without complaint, my initial dismay and vexation gradually faded, replaced by patience and humor. I rejoiced to have my mother at my side, completely lucid, her gentle, loving self at the ripe age of ninety plus. I learned to care for her while respecting her dignity and honoring her limited independence. The transitional process took several months, not to mention considerable soul searching on my part.

Between January and May of 1994, I made three trips to Tuscany to spend weeks at a time with my mother. She had reached the impressive age of 94 and though she still played a wicked game of scrabble, physically she was becoming frailer. We had always been convinced that she would reach her 100th birthday, surrounded by the entire the family, biological, adopted, spanning three generations.

In early July, I flew across the Atlantic for the fourth time that year. My aunt, who had retired at the same time and shared our country home, had warned me to expect a shocking change. Mother had been confined to her bed for almost two months, victim of a devastating flu, and was growing weaker by the day.

The hour-long drive from the Florence airport sped by

in a flash. I braced myself before crossing the threshold of the upper loggia that led into the house. Mother was dozing when I tiptoed into her room. Still several feet from her bedside, I paused to take in the aura of tranquility that suffused her inner sanctum. I tried to capture within a single sweeping glance her fine white hair, the lovely curve of her cheek, the familiar high forehead, surprisingly free of wrinkles since her recent weight loss and her slight form that barely made a ripple in the bed. Perhaps sensing my presence, her eyes opened and her face lit up as she exclaimed, "Darling, at last!"

I had longed to be at my mother's side from the moment she had shown the first signs of weakening, but was bound by teaching and family obligations to remain an ocean apart. For the ensuing three weeks, however, I assumed total responsibility for Mother's care, freeing up my aunt, herself well into her eighties.

I quickly set aside any incipient anxiety as I prepared to make Mother as comfortable as possible. I installed a hospital bed and had it outfitted with a water-cooled mattress and washable sheepskin to keep her from developing bedsores.

Though Mother professed that she was never hungry, I spent hours in our tiny kitchen, chopping, peeling, slicing, stirring, and blending colors and flavors into her favorite dishes. I poured all the culinary expertise I had acquired from her over the years into faint replicas of her past creations. A great chef in her heyday, Mother was one of those rare people who could read any recipe and actually "taste" the finished product! Even as her appetite declined, she still cared about flavor.

I pureed all food and presented it in minute amounts for fear that the mere sight of a full plate would be overwhelming. I invested such passion and faith in these daily creations, always embellished by a miniature bouquet, a single rose or a sprig of lavender, that I never doubted their healing power. I would silently will my mother to take just one more bite, one more sip, in hopes that the extra morsel would increase her strength. When at length the requested menus dwindled to one of two choices, freshly made eggnog or tapioca pudding, I rejoiced over the steady intake of calcium and protein while senselessly fretting about her cholesterol levels.

At first, sharp-witted and alert as ever, Mother welcomed our quiet chats as a change of pace and a pleasant distraction. Formerly a brilliant conversationalist and storyteller, she now preferred to listen. Due to her increasing deafness, she had been outfitted with hearing aids to enable her to remain in touch with the outside world. But she found them cumbersome and often dismissed them with a flourish, often hiding them under her pillow.

As the days slipped by, our exchanges became fewer and further between. More often than not, I would find that Mother was dozing when I entered her room. I would quietly steal away unnoticed, loath to interrupt what I believed to be restorative sleep. There seemed little need to talk, all having been said and resolved long since.

My daughter joined me from Paris where she was studying and offered comfort, relaxing massages and daily bouquets of variegated pungent wild flowers, which Mother accepted with a smile and inhaled as life itself.

It was a privilege for both of us, side by side, to tend to my mother's daily requirements, to learn by watching her contend with the iniquities of old age, in her stoic yet gracious manner. I was aware that in her own way, she was preparing for her final journey. Her dignity intact, her pride and sense of humor never faltered.

What touched me most, when granted the luxury to reflect, was the aura of other worldliness about my mother, the equanimity and almost tangible spirituality that emanated from her person. As I gazed upon her in silence, I dwelt upon what made her unique: her special blend of oriental wisdom and western pragmatism, her invincible spirit and resilience in the face of adversity and personal tragedy (of which she had had more than her share), her love of adventure, her profound humanity that touched all who knew her and lastly, her ability to laugh at herself.

Far too soon, the time for my departure snuck up on me. Over the course of the previous two years and frequent trips to Tuscany, as the moment approached to pack my bags, I had had to steel myself when bidding Mother a final goodnight. Each time, as I drifted off to sleep, I prayed that she would find the strength and will to stay alive until my next visit.

This time, however, I left with a light heart as I planned to return within five weeks, just before the new term began at Harvard. After a quick hug and kiss, a reassuring "I will be back before you know it!" I sped off towards the Florence airport.

After my return to the States, not a day went by without calling my aunt. Mother seemed profoundly content. She was holding her own, though eating less and less until she began to refuse all food, including her favorite eggnogs. All she craved was clear, fresh water. She also appeared to be sleeping most of the time, though when roused, was happy to chat and always inquired about the children and me.

About a week later, the phone rang. It was my aunt. She could barely speak. Mother had passed away, peacefully and painlessly in the middle of the night. When my aunt found her in the morning, snuggled down off to one corner of the bed, a smile upon her lips, she looked as though she were merely sleeping. Freed from all bodily needs and constraints, released from the emotional bond of my presence, Mother had become pure spirit.

I brought my mother's ashes back to Vermont where my aunt had purchased a two-hundred-year-old farmhouse in 1939. The children, my aunt and I buried her in the old cemetery on Acton Hill, mostly populated by gravesites dating back to the late 1800's. We waited three years to perform our private ceremony, taking turns at digging the appropriate sized hole in our little family plot, set off in the far left-hand corner of the graveyard, partially shaded by towering pines and white birches, partially bathed in dappled sunlight. We shared fond memories as the shovel sank into the rich dark loam, releasing the earthy aroma of freshly exposed soil. At times we laughed, especially when the handling of the urn gave forth a gentle tinkling from the titanium of mother's hip replacements. "She is speaking to us." On our walk to the cemetery, my daughter had filled a basket with multicolored wild flowers we lovingly set next to the simple granite marker that bore my mother's name and dates: Elsa Oiesen Bement, 1900-1994.

Though I began to mourn my mother's death long before she actually passed away, hoping that it would prepare me for what I knew would be an almost unbearable loss, it only helped in a minor way. I was still teaching full time, and increasingly caring for my daredevil aunt whose indomitable spirit belied her age. Mother's death had the effect of stripping away some of the protective layers that had stilled in me the need to know not only any information I could find on my natural mother and father, though all records were sealed and my adoption had been highly secret, but also about Mother's family history and connections to her past, going back to Denmark, China and Korea. Years of research and travel have gone into my dual quest. This is neither the time nor place to reveal the seemingly insurmountable obstacles I had to overcome nor share the astounding discoveries. Readers will have to curb their curiosity until my two memoirs in progress finally appear in print form.

I have chosen to address the stereotype of the adoptee as a perpetual child by telling parts of my own story. Though many adopted individuals are haunted throughout their lives by their initial losses, of their natural family, their heritage, their lack of a sense of belonging, and become consumed by continuous rage, anger, even suicidal thoughts or worse, others like myself have been blessed with truly loving families and unique role models.

My Mother, though not adopted, experienced being torn from her native land and culture, separated from her beloved parents for years at a time. Part of her understanding of my feelings, though never openly expressed, came from her own childhood. That she was able to overcome loneliness, homesickness and the yearning to be close to her parents, especially when they most needed her, and instead reached out to the world, embracing not only me as her very own, but countless others, and then let us fly away, only to return time and again, set the course of my life journey.

I used to quietly recite to myself, when thinking of Mother: "If you live be a hundred, I want to live to be a hundred minus one day, so I never have to live without you"—Winnie the Pooh, A.A. Milne, 1926. To this day, my mother walks by my side, is ever present, in death as in life, a constant inspiration and challenge. I greet each day with renewed commitment and gratitude.

# Angela Tucker

## SHOULD ADOPTEES BE CONSIDERED A GIFT?

A LL OF MY LIFE, PEOPLE began conversations to me with statements like, "Your parents are amazing!" My schoolteachers and doctors, my friends and their parents, even grocery store clerks made this statement to me, as they watched our multi-racial, special needs, rambunctious family shuttle to and from different places around the town of Bellingham, Washington. The context behind this statement was generally folks expressing their disbelief in conjunction with awe and reverence for my parents' choice to adopt so many children with special needs. As an adult, I find myself searching through my brain in an effort to address this statement in a kind, yet impactful way that may have an effect (however slight) on the person. I seek to answer in a way that is not condescending, but is informative and stern. This may well describe the plight of adult adoptees; walking a thin line of balancing others' expectations with their true reality. They seek to conform, yet are often pummeled with statements that infer inferiority or force us to receive "praise" as though we are recently adopted children, needing to be rescued. My thoughts often circle back to the rhetorical question, is there something so wrong with all of us that only "amazing" parents could handle? Were there any other "amazing" people who would've been willing to adopt us?

In the midst of my existential adoptee dilemmas, I find solace in knowing that my parents parented their children as they would any other child, and they now view me as an adult as any other parent would view their adult daughter. They viewed what others termed as "special needs" or "disabled" as *an* aspect of our person-hood, but not *the* aspect of our person-hood. They entered into complex and difficult situations, yet were aware and hopeful of our resilience and strength within the realm of abilities and disabilities as well as other areas of our lives, hobbies and interests. They recognized that our needs were not limited to those labels in the DSM or the need for an IEP or 504 plan, but rather our realities due to difficult beginnings, of which adoption is obviously a facet.

When people hear the word adoption, visions of highly capable, well-dressed, educated and childless couples come to mind- couples that are yearning to parent a baby. This image is troubling as not only does it not center on the adoptee, but rather it focuses in on a need of the hopeful adoptive parents, and the hole that the adoptee will supposedly fill. Is this hole still filled as the baby grows into a teen, and adulthood? The concept of an adult adoptee is lost on many. The issues of abandonment, identity, self-esteem troubles and fear of intimacy that often plague adoptees in their adulthood is lost, as the focus for the general public remains centered around the new adoptive parents' little bundle of joy, and what a "great deed" they have done.

The adoptee routinely hears comments such as "You are such a gift to your parents," or "You should feel lucky that you were hand-selected/chosen." These comments, aside from the bleeding ignorance, leave no room for a rebuttal. I was never able to counter the statement to a non-adopted friend, with "Are you sad that you weren't placed in a new environment without consent, and then chosen by a 'better' 'more suitable' parent?" or a rebuttal to a friends' parent (of a biological child) with "Don't you want to give a gift (their child) to someone to make their lives happier?" In the same way that these arguments have no merit, others' comments to adoptees are also baseless. The loss of an adoptee's birth parents (no matter what age this occurs, infancy to late teens) will forever leave an imprint on the adoptee in some shape or fashion. When this fact is overlooked or dismissed, it furthers the adoptee's sense of needing to be grateful, to be silent and to attribute their feelings of sadness to something other than their adoptee status.

I am thankful to have been afforded opportunities, to have a strong intact family and to have the space to understand the meaning of different life experiences. I'm not thankful because I was adopted, but I'm thankful because I am part of a large, diverse and wonderful family. These two events, though closely related, are not inextricably tied together. They are separate, yet equally important, character-shaping events that have made me into the adult adoptee I am today. I am *not* a gift.

# April Topfer

*Perhaps every adoptee bears within himself the imprint of a special or unique spiritual vocation. It is spiritual. It is always spiritual... the matter of the heart and soul... The mystery of adoption is that the adoptee was truly, as Betty Jean Lifton has said, twice born... born first of the flesh and then again in the spirit.* (Severson, as cited in Schooler, 1995, p. 25)

ALTHOUGH THE ADOPTED INDIVIDUAL IS "twice born" (Lifton, 1983, p. 5)—first of the flesh and then of the spirit—we have no ritual ceremonies, initiations, or rites of passage in the closed adoption system to ensure that the adopted individual's spirit has successfully joined the body. Mythology scholar and historian Eliade et al. (1984) explained that *initiation* is "a body of rites and oral teachings whose purpose is to produce a decisive alteration in the religious and social status of the person to be initiated" (p. x). Therefore, the initiate becomes another person—more fully in life emotionally and more spiritually aware.

Loss of identity and even feeling betrayal of one's self are essential to rites of passages. Initiation is a universal right and an archetypal form that surfaces and influences life wherever events have the spirit of beginning or the weight of ending (Eliade et al., 1984). Ethnographer van Gennep (1960) defined *rites of passage* as having three major phases: separation, transition, and incorporation. From these definitions, initiation and rites of passage are naturally embedded in adoption by fact of its circumstantial nature, however, not all rites of passage are developed to the same extent—"they may be reduced to a minimum in adoption" (van Gennep, 1960, p. viii). Overall, initiations and rites of passage are conducted with the intention of initiating one's true spirit, Essence, and soul into the physical body. The goal is to develop autonomy and transform. Because there are no conscious or intentional initiations or rites of passage in closed adoptions, adopted individuals not only suffer the many loses of their identities and of their biological lineage, they also lose the most natural union between flesh and spirit. Adoption belongs with the great spiritual disciplines of every age whose work is a work against nature (Severson, 1994).

Due to the closed adoption system's ignorance of initiations and rites of passages the adopted individual's recognition of the natural union between flesh and spirit is not immediately available. Autonomy takes time, work, and energy until a consistent and balanced interplay between spirit and flesh happens. When the time becomes ripe, the union can be consummated, creating a strong embodied container for growth, autonomy, and transformation. In closed adoptions, however, the strong container for union is not possible for the child because the adopted person is left with many ungrieved losses, splits, and holes. A hole is nothing but an absence of a certain part of our Essence that one feels in the body as emptiness—something is wrong and something is lacking (Almaas, 1990). We try to fill the hole and turn to external influences to guide our autonomy. Thus, the soul and spirit are disconnected and lost.

Lifton (1994) discussed the losses in adopted individuals as a split between the authentic identity versus the "Forbidden Self" (p. 56). One sees the split between the flesh and the spirit. One is embraced and one is effaced, one is viewed as real, the other is banned as inauthentic. Thus, the child who was once so full of love never becomes an adult full of life (Severson, 1994). He is not an autonomous individual with soul and spirit. The child's energy is instead directed toward perpetuating and filling the holes that the legacy of the closed adoption system left behind. Thus, the adult lives in a perpetual child state.

In this discussion, the author proposes that the lack of conscious and intentional initiatory conceptions in the closed adoption system leaves the adopted individual in a perpetual state of childhood. However, the adult adopted person can set out to create his own initiatory conceptions involving intention, consciousness, and awareness. Initiatory conceptions are a series of conscious initiations to join the flesh and the spirit together to create a strong container for Essence, soul, and spirit to enter the body and call the body home, in other words, to experience conscious *embodiment*. Embodiment is experiencing being, "in the lived-body" (Marrone, 1990, p. xii), from moment to moment, sensing precisely those body-sensations, feelings, and thoughts which give form to the sense-of-self. The embodied body holds the autonomous spirit.

The author will explore how the adopted individual can use initiatory conceptions as a means for psychospiritual work and development for the adopted individual. Part of the work is engaging in a conscious and intentional process of listening and hearing the deeper messages about one's adoption reflected in the adoption story, identity, and significant developmental stages on the adoption path. This becomes a process of transformation—light can shine on the holes and other dark places that are felt in the body and the perpetual child's spirit and soul can be retrieved, managed, and integrated to make a strong autonomous container for the flesh and spirit to interconnect and join together.

To explore the psychospiritual development of adopted individuals, the author will use a transpersonal psychological lens. *Transpersonal psychology* is an integrative and holistic approach to psychology that studies phenomena beyond the ego (Hartelius, Caplan, and Rardin, 2007). Transpersonal psychology addresses "the full spectrum of human psychospiritual development—from our deepest wounds and needs, to the existential crisis of the human being, to the most transcendent capacities of our consciousness" (Caplan, 2009, p. 231). The word psychospiritual integrates the psychological and the spiritual aspects of an individual. Psychospiritual additionally includes one's bodily presence, awareness, and integration. A psychospiritual developmental model for adopted individuals is well-suited because adoption is a lifelong journey of discovering the self for the adopted individual (Brodzinsky, et al.). "Adoption naturally carries the adoptee into a unique form of spiritual-psychological reality" (Severson, 1994, p. 8).

Opportunities for conscious and intentional initiations, or initiatory conceptions, as the author will refer them as, along the adoption path will be highlighted in the following sections. Opportunities for initiatory conceptions set the stage for autonomous embodiment and the interplay between spirit and flesh. They also bring the phases of separation, transition, and integration with them; they set into motion the adult adopted individual's work of psychospiritual development, transformation, and growth. By listening to the deeper messages of the body and discovering an embodied spirituality, the body's container becomes strong and autonomous and the perpetual child's spirit and soul can be *rebirthed* to join the flesh.

In the first section, the author will share her own voice and her research findings that explored traditional and nontraditional mindfulness practices among adult adopted. The second section will suggest a series of initiatory conceptions found on an adopted individual's path that she can use to grow and transform–the embryonic phase, initiation of the adoption story, and the naturally embedded initiation of search and reunion. The last section will include concluding remarks about the stages of transitions and integration in initiations and what adopted individuals need to watch out for so they don't get stuck on the adoption path.

Before moving forward, there is one last important clarification. The author will use concepts such as *patriarchal, feminine, conscious femininity*, etc. These terms are not meant to exclude men from the discussion. On the contrary—feminine energies are also found in men and masculine energies are found in the female psyche. I know adult adopted men who are embarking on a conscious spiritual path and who are subsequently engaging in forms of conscious initiatory practices to help move the energy of their adoption journeys toward psychospiritual growth and transformation. In addition, when the author speaks about a strong and autonomous feminine container for one's body—in which the perpetual child's spirit and soul have a safe place to land—the author is referring to the feminine principle, which male bodies have full access as well.

Regardless of gender, a receptive body that invites and takes in the child's lost spirit and soul is considered to be more feminine in nature. Thus, comparing the *conscious feminine* perspective to the current discussion, the task of conscious initiatory conceptions and psychospiritual development is about releasing the gentler and unconditionally compassionate and loving feminine from the tyrannical power of the driven, crazed masculine—which the closed adoption system perpetuates. Conscious initiatory conceptions then are not only about consummating the flesh and the spirit but about balancing the feminine and masculine principles in an autonomous and harmonious state. As Woodman (1992) wrote, "Conscious femininity is grounded enough to relate to the divine without identifying with it; conscious masculinity is discriminating enough to cut identification with a sharp sword. Identification is unconscious; relationship is conscious." (p. 14).

## Autobiographical Voice

Because I grew up in a closed adoption, conscious initiatory conceptions were not part of the fabric of my family's life. There were many opportune times that my parents could have engaged in some intentional and conscious conversation but instead, they chose to bury the truth and embrace and fortify the "secrecy of silence" (Lifton, 1994, p. 10). The dark silence felt smothering and I could not individuate. My parents pretended that my older adoptive sister and I were their biological children. Thus, I was left to conform my body to others who did not understand or recognize my own flesh and my spirit's individual container. Johnson (1992) reminded us that from infancy through old age we are taught to conform our bodies from external cues. We are rewarded for keeping quiet and controlling our bodily impulses:

The implied meaning of these recurrent nonverbal messages is consistent with the explicit teachings: our bodies, with their feelings, impulses, and perceptions, are not to be trusted, and must be subjected to external controls to keep them from leading us astray. They must be trained to support the status quo. (p. 33)

Status quo was where my child's body and spirit shallowly operated from, assuming I only came from my parents but as many adopted persons have also stated, I felt uncomfortable because something was missing.

Due to the status quo of secrecy, the work of deciphering the hidden and mysterious unknown codes of how my spirit and my body was interconnected was left solely up to me. There were no breadcrumb trails about how to manage all the changes, emotions, and flavors that my body experienced, and I could not take cues from those around me about my biological features, characteristics, and identity. At most times I was miserable at managing myself. The more I tried to manage the holes left in my body from the lack of initiations, the more they seemed to grow—matching the diameter to how far my spirit moved away from my body. I was dependent on the closed system for giving me this life.

Dark places were even noticeable on my skin, with several larger freckles and birthmarks, in which I automatically projected my birthright differences onto when I was around 13 years old. Severson (1979) stated that the *puer aeternus*—the archetype of the eternal child—lives in special relationship to the organ of the skin. *Archetypes* are styles of consciousness, patterns of behavior, and forms of fantasy. The puer chooses the skin because the skin is in many ways the most visible of the organs and the puer demands that her wounds be open and visible for all to see. Although the lens through which I perceived my biological differences was distorted and negatively targeted my skin, the dis-ease of my adoption was visibly apparent in how my psyche and spirit interacted with my body. My child's soul was sending messages about how much my biological differences affected me but in a way that was acceptable and hidden in the status quo of silence. As a result, my split and dark places remained unprocessed and any conscious and successful passages of initiation involving recognition of my autonomous biological body and its spirit were lost.

Another lost initiation opportunity came when I began my menstruation—what I like to call my *moon cycle.* Eliade (1984) confirmed that female initiations are related to the mystery of blood and that it begins with the first menstruation. My moon cycle happened early when I was 10 years old, which I'm aware that other adopted girls also experience at a young age due to living with a non-biologically related man. I felt immense shame and self-consciousness about it at the time and tried to hide it from everyone, although I was unsuccessful when my blood soaked through my pants at school. Was my body sending out the message that my hidden blood in my adoption could no longer be contained in its façade and status quo? Shuttle and Redgrove (1986) claimed that every child experiences his mother's menstruation, whether he knows it or not. I didn't consciously recognize that I had inherited not only her flow of blood but probably the PMS and stomach cramps that came along with my moon cycle as well.

My blood of kin was not given conscious or autonomous recognition in my closed adoption and neither was my moon cycle. I did not have my matriarchal kin to reflect and mirror my moon cycle back to me, something my biological sisters and my first/birth mother would have naturally provided me. I am aware that this notion sounds romantic, however, no one romanticizes blood relationships more than a person who has never known them (Lifton, 1994); women's initiation is important for all women in adulthood and autonomy but especially true for adopted women. We cannot know or understand who we are as women and what our bodies are capable of.

In his classic book *Rites and Symbols of Initation,* Eliade (1984) explained that female initiation is performed collectively, under the direction of the older female relatives—as in India—or of old women—as is the case in Africa. He wrote,

These tutoresses instruct the younger women in the secrets of sexuality and fertility, and teach them the customs of the tribe and at least some of its religious traditions—those accessible to women. The education thus given is general, but its essence is religious; it consists in a revelation of the sacrality of women. The girl is ritually prepared to assume her specific mode of being, that is, to become a creatress, and at the same time is taught her responsibilities which, among primitives, are always religious in nature. (p. 42)

Additionally, the initiand would be immediately isolated, separated from the community during this initial initiation, something that I naturally desire when I get my moon cycle every month. Pregnant women were also isolated from society in order for the mother and child to be safe and later to be reintroduced in stages (van Gennep, 1960).

Aside from the loss of the initiatory passage for my first moon cycle, when I turned 16 years old I literally lost my voice. I did not know my natural voice and its rhythms and tempo because the closed adoption and its status quo of silence rendered my voice silent. My inner voice and my body reflected and mirrored what was being given to me by the external—stay dependent upon the closed system for your life. Women's researcher Gilligan (1993) stated, "Voice is natural and also cultural. It is composed of breath and sound, words, rhythm, and language. And voice is a powerful psychological instrument and channel, connecting inner and outer worlds" (p. xvi). My natural voice and my breath were not in sync with my child's spirit and soul. My body and voice naturally wanted to achieve autonomy but the closed system doesn't teach me how to be independent.

The status quo of silence left my body so weak, thus,

my child was forced to find her own way of engaging in initiation—smoking cigarettes. Albeit my choice in smoking was not the best one, however, the act of smoke does provide an outline of invisible ghosts. Perhaps my child thought smoking would serve two purposes—filling in the holes of my throat, chest, and lungs where the lack of openness in communication branded its mark and to outline the ghosts of my adoption.

Lifton (1994) claimed there are many ghosts in the adopted family's room. There are the birth children that the adoptive family might have had, and there are the first/birth parents. Smoking for me could then outline "The Ghost Kingdom" (p. 57) and help me to resolve the split loyalties between the loyalty I felt toward my adoptive parents who rescued me and the invisible loyalty to my mother who gave birth to me. Due to all the unspoken ghosts in my family and the lack of openness, no wonder my father suffered and died of esophagus cancer several years ago.

Needless to say, smoking cigarettes did not provide the solution for my split loyalties or lack of autonomy. If anything, smoking became a double-edged sword for my spirit and soul to swallow. On one side cigarettes provided my child self with an intimate *I-Thou* relationship. Cigarettes were my meditation, my best friend, something that I could always count on. My ghosts from the *Ghost Kingdom* were amplified but not until years later when I began to consciously inquire into my adoption and begin engagement in a series of psychospiritual initiations. The other side of the sword of smoking caused my body uncomfortable pain and suffering. Smoking was artificial, fake, and toxic—things that were identical to the closed adoption system. I later resolved to quit the charade of smoke and mirrors of my closed adoption and discover healthier ways to initiate my body and spirit in conscious connection.

Quitting smoking was not as easy as my adult self imagined, however. My child was terrified because what was the identity of this new person who doesn't smoke? Where would the child fit in if the body was strong enough for spirit and soul? I eventually quit after 20 odd years of engaging in my addiction. I tell people for as long as I smoked, was as long as it took me to stop. As I later found out after I quit that perhaps some of my difficulty in quitting was that my first/birth father smokes and has for years. His mother still occasionally smokes and his deceased father was a chain-smoker. Smoking is not the only thing my first/birth father and I have in common. We also feel a strong connection with the transpersonal, although his fascination is about parapsychology—a subset topic of transpersonal psychology.

At the time I was trying to quit smoking and looking for a dissertation research topic I was practicing mediation, specifically Vipassana meditation—or what is commonly known in our western culture as mindfulness meditation. Mindfulness meditation is modeled after insight meditation in the Theravada Buddhist tradition and means "paying attention in a particular way: on purpose, in the present moment, and nonjudgmentally" (Kabat-Zinn, 1994, p. 4). I participated in several silent retreats, day long meditations, weekly meditation sits, and an 8-week secularized mindfulness meditation class called Mind Body Stress Reduction (MBSR; Kabat-Zinn, 1990). Over the course of several years I learned to disidentify from and deconstruct my dysfunctional attachment with the closed adoption system. Disidentification from my thoughts, feelings, and sensations became part of my practice. False beliefs and attitudes about how I *should* and *ought* to be were revealed and came under a microscope to be examined.

The practice of nonattachment became an intense and profound practice for me because I began to shed light on my adoptive identity. As a result, I inversely began to fully embrace my adoptive identity and not deny myself the truth about my adoption experience; this was my initiatory conception. The transformation from my old identity to my new one provided me a lot of relief, and I soon felt feelings of belonging and was able to paradoxically let go of my adoptive identity.

Meditation teacher Engler's (2003) famous epigram reflected my disindentification process: "You have to be somebody before you can be nobody" (p. 35). In other words, because I had the intention to fully embrace my adoptive identity, my child's fear of letting go of the ambiguous and false identity that was created in my closed adoption began unraveling and demonstrate more of the truth of who I am—spirit, Essence, and soul. My autonomy and silence was deepened and the dark holes and spaces in my body were being witnessed with curiosity and empathy, not with automaticity and unconsciousness.

### Research: Adult Adopted Women's Mindfulness Experiences

The initiatory conception of deconstructing my old identity and embracing my adoptive identity involved a series of psychospiritual practices to get in touch with my voice. I told others about being adopted and the work I was doing. I brought more transparency about my adoptive identity and spoke about the importance of adoption in my life—something I dared not utter growing up. I wrote about my experience of finding voice and how the process of discovering my "conscious femininity" (Woodman, 1992, p. 12) and feminist voice was, and can be for other adopted women, a catalyst for psychospiritual growth and transformation (see Topfer, 2010).

During this time I also decided on my research topic. I was curious to know if other adopted women had similar experiences such as mine on their adoption paths. Intuitive inquiry was the research method I chose because it allowed me as researcher to explore topics that ignite enthusiasm, to honor life experiences as sources of inspiration, and to invite the research process to transform my understanding of the topic and life (Anderson, 2000). Although I was biting off a lot by exploring a topic that was profoundly personal and using a qualitative method to personally unravel and explore my worldview, beliefs, values, assumptions, and feelings about adoption, I couldn't fathom any other topic that would interest me more. I still can't. Thus, I used my dissertation research with its qualitative approach to form a series of psychospiritual initiations to deepen my process and lived-experience about my adoption. In addition, I journaled intensely about my experiences. Journaling became a series of initiatory passage in itself. Writing freely held a place of refuge, comfort, and connection that I could trust and confide in.

For my dissertation research, I explored the psychospiritual health and well-being of 10 adult adopted women. I asked the women about their adoption experiences growing up in closed adoptions, their traditional and nontraditional mindfulness practices, and their relationships. The women had various practices and exercises, such as meditation, yoga, swimming, journaling, prayer, dance, and/or creative expression. Interestingly, all the women who had explored their adoptions by either attending peer-led adoption support groups, and/or adoption-related conferences, and/or had been in some phase of search and reunion, stated somewhere during the interview that their journey, practice, and experiences were *spiritual*. The 2 women who had not explored their adoptions nor who had not been in search and reunion did not refer to anything in their lives as *spiritual* and had not presented their stories in a coherent manner.

Overall, I concluded that mindfulness had been helpful and used as a complimentary tool for adopted women to explore their adoptions. They found that by engaging in their spiritual and mindfulness practices, they were able to experience more focus and awareness, open curiosity, and a sense of letting go and acceptance about their experiences. It appeared then that mindfulness helped these women cultivate a different way of how they processed, held, and reacted to their adoption experiences. Cultivating mindful awareness was thus seen as a way for adopted women to help integrate their adoption experiences on their path of psychospiritual development, health, and well-being.

## Psychospiritual Development: A Series of Initiatory Conceptions

> *The double who is the other possible self remains forever infantilized. It is always the abandoned baby. When the Adoptee goes back to search for it, it is still there, frozen in time, at the same age he left it to begin his other life.* (Clothier, as cited in Lifton, p. 35)

The eternal child, also known as the *puer aeternus*, is the archetype of the perpetual child who has never grown up. He is given two options for growth—either work or birthing and raising his own child(ren) (von Franz, 1981). In the latter, we have seen the transformative effects on adopted individuals when they have birthed their own biological children. The other option—psychospiritual work—is to reclaim the perpetual child's soul and spirit by building and mending a strong container for all the holes and splits in the psyche and body. Thus, despite being due undeniable recognition and celebration of their births, adopted individuals have the opportunity to not only be *twice born* but *thrice born* when the flesh and spirit are consummated and joined in union. The act of this embodied marriage involves conscious initiatory conceptions on an adopted person's path; full engagement with the body, resulting in an "embodied spirituality" (Woodman, 1990, p. 98).

Initiatory conceptions have three phases: separation, transition, and incorporation, and can be found in many different forms. Some involve different spiritual practices such as meditation and yoga, and others such as creative expression and writing that involve the use of one's voice as a means of finding one's "inner mystic" (Feldman, 2005, p. 34). Whichever form of conscious initiation the individual engages in, the body's messages and deeper wisdom become the central focus of the work and the intentional vehicle for healing and transformation. Engaging in an initiatory practice on one's conscious adoption path allows many possibilities of growth if one opens up to one owns one's bodily rhythms (Shuttle and Redgrove, 1978). Accordingly, as the adopted individual begins to recognize and allure more meaning from her adoption, her psyche can clue her in as to where her perpetual child is still separated from spirit and soul and how to begin the process of retrieving them back. The ultimate goal then is to reclaim her true identity and autonomous spirit in spite of being raised in a closed adoption.

If one can begin to imagine then that the status quo of closed adoptions is a dis-ease for the child, then one can see the similarities between adoption being a lifelong journey and the natural path toward psychospiritual development and growth for an adopted individual. Mindell (1985) reflected, "A chronic disease is often a lifelong problem, a part of someone's individuation process. I don't believe that a person actually creates disease, but that his soul is expressing an important message to him through the disease" (p. 13). C. G. Jung stressed that the process of *individuation,* constitutes the ultimate goal of human life. Individuation is accomplished through a series of ordeals of initiatory type. In modern times, the Hero is proved, among other things, by the presence of initiatory themes in the dreams and imaginative activity of modern man (Eliade, 1984).

Like initiations and rites of passages, adoption also involves individuation for the adopted person. Individuation is interchangeable and involves a series of psychospiritual practices and initiatory conceptions with autonomy and wholeness as goals. There is tremendous suffering that the process of individuation touches, however, and it can cause a tremendous wound because, put simply, we are robbed of the capacity for arranging our own lives according to our own wishes. "Having been overprotected by their adoptive parents and disempowered by society, adoptees know more about being the eternal child than about being a mother or father" (Lifton, p. 118). The perpetual child wants to be an autonomous spirit but fears the consequence of being abandoned again. The unconscious mother and closed system do not want to change (Woodman, 1992).One can conclude then that the psychospiritual development for an adopted adult involves re-mothering one's self (Zweig, 1990).

### Birth of the Flesh: Reclaiming the Darkness

*The disheartening truth is that the psychological importance of being adopted does not recede in adulthood... but lies waiting to take center stage at various transitions in the life cycle* (Lifton, 1994, p. 110).

Jungian analyst and writer Estes (2012) explained that ritual makes a protective shelter for the soul. At the time of an adopted individual's birth, she did not have a celebratory ritual or homecoming for her spirit and flesh to become one. The child's authentic flesh was not mirrored and the spirit experienced what Estes (2012) called *susto*. *Susto* is the term used to explain an infant's soul fright because adoption is a sudden change in one's life. Estes suggested one calls out to the soul "Little Angel," in high hopes that the spirit will eventually return to the body. Because closed adoptions do not provide iron-clad rituals to protect the adopted child's soul, everyone tip-toes around the adopted individual, reinforcing the fragility of her psyche. No one dares to stomp their foot down until much later when the perpetual child is suffering from everyone's fear.

Later in life, engagement of intentional rituals and initiatory conceptions on one's adoption path becomes vital for the retrieval of the perpetual child's autonomous spirit and soul. The closed system will always keep the child trapped if the adult doesn't do something about it. But again, the lack of initiatory conceptions keeps the adopted individual never feeling fully rooted, ever really born of earth (Severson, 1994). "Without that interplay between spirit and body, the spirit is always trapped" (Woodman, 1982, p. 16). The goal is not only the integration of spirit and matter but the realization that not only does one not exist without the other but that one is the other in a different form (Woodman, 1992).

Moreover, developmental psychologist Piaget theorized that a child's experience of the world begins with the body and the symbolism of the body, however, the adopted child's birth did not create positive images nor symbols of the flesh at the time of separation. Instead, the closed adoption birthed an ominous and smothering "conspiracy of silence" (Lifton, 1994, p. 10) that created "an erasure of details that might contradict what could be read or seen about the body" (Leighton, 2005, p. 163), thus, reinforcing the lack of independence and autonomous spirit. As many adopted individuals have felt, no matter how lost to them their natural parents may be, the adopted child carries stamped in every cell of his body genes derived from his forebearers (Clothier, as cited in Lifton, 1982).

The authentic cells and genes are the materials of the dark matter in the body. The perpetual child continues to guard over the darkness because no one else, especially the closed adoption system, is willing to shed light on the darkness. Furthermore, Wellich (as cited in Lifton, 1983) explained the importance of the body being mirrored. The *body image*—describes a picture of our own body which also extends beyond its confines:

> As a matter of fact persons outside ourselves are essential for the development of our complete body-image. The most important persons in this respect are our real parents and other members of our family. Knowledge of and definite relationship to his genealogy is therefore necessary for a child to build up his complete body-image and world picture. (p. 48)

Not only does the *body image* extend to include the shadows of the body but the shadow was regarded by indigenous people as an actual part of the body (Wellich, as cited in Lifton, 1983).

In general, shadows have considerable psychological significance on the psychic body. They are part of the body's container and when found and worked through with mindful intention of allowing their true nature to be revealed, the shadows can contribute to the healing pot for the perpetual child's soul and spirit. In addition to creating a strong and solid container, part of an adopted person's psychospiritual work is to create a larger pot for the dark parts of the psyche to exist in harmony with spirit and creatively flow. The perception of the darkness is light in the darkness: it is the beginning of healing (Woodman, 1992). Images in dreams or in different forms of meditation and somatic work can shine light and join together with the dark.

Yoga is a good example of combining the light and

the dark in the body's container because yoga literally means to bind together, to hold fast, and to yoke (Eliade, 1990). Eliade (1984) considers Yoga be the best possible initiatory theme for reevaluating traditional initiatory themes. He wrote,

> Not only does the outward aspect of Yoga practice suggest the behavior of a novice during his initiatory training; for the yogi forsakes the company of men, withdraws into solitude, submits to a course of ascetic practices that are sometimes extremely severe,and puts himself under the oral teaching of a master ... the corpus of Yoga practices reproduces an initiatorypattern. (p. 106)

The symbolism of initiatory death is clearly discernible in the various psychophysiological techniques in Yoga. "If we watch a yogi while he is practicing Yoga, we get the impression that his is trying in every way to do exactly the opposite of what is done 'in the world,' that is, what men do *as men*, prisoners of their own ignorance" (Eliade, 1984, p. 106).

Part of the initiatory practice of adopted adults is n*ot to do what the closed system has done unto them.* The perpetual child can become more conscious about how the closed adoption system has been trapped as repetitive body patterns in the body; one practice to initiate psychospiritual transformation is to focus on the breath. Breath is an inborn potential to regain the lost spirit of one's natural bodily rhythms and movements. "Natural breathing" (Lewis, 1997, p. 17) is a capability that we had as babies and young children but lost as adults. Part of the child's spirit is found in the natural breath. The loss of our breath demonstrates itself in mental experiences and they reflect, as they oftentimes do, bodily ones (Shuttle and Redgrove, 1986). In yoga, breath is called *pranayama—*

restraint and ethical observance of vital energy (Rosen, 2002). The conscious initiation of breath thus entails the intentional practice and observance of energy in the body.

Unfortunately, the adopted individual could have a lifetime of constricting and unconsciously holding his or her breath, resulting in chronic shallow breathing. Arising out of this constriction could be unresolved loss and grief which could result in symptoms of trauma or addictive behavior which ultimately demonstrate the unconscious specialization and perfection in the patriarchal culture we live in (Woodman, 1982). When patterns such as these are unrealized, the transition of genuine growth from childhood to adulthood remains dormant in the body (Bentzen, et al., 2004) and can become muscularly frozen to a particular emotional pattern. Thus, the body remains predisposed to experiencing those feelings connected with that emotion (Marrone, 1990) unless the feminine is firmly connected to the musculature of the body and experiences the visceral affirmation that says, "This is of value to me. This is who I am." (Woodman, 1992, p. 12). This type of affirmation not only mirrors the rhythms and dark energies of the closed adoption system that are trapped in the adopted person's body but additionally causes the light and the dark to be integrated and incorporated in the body.

### Embryonic Return to the Great Mother

*The adoptee regresses as time regresses. One is on a 'pilgrimage back to the womb,' as one adoptee put it, moving toward one's mother* (Lifton, 1994, p.144).

Eliade (1984) stated that initiation is the symbolic transformation into an embryo. Embryonic gestation marks the phase of transition and incorporation. Before the transformation happens, the initiand is still considered unborn. True rebirth only happens when the person's spirit and soul can be consciously united and joined. Initiation then is a *spiritual rebirth* of the autonomous embodiment of flesh and spirit. Whether the adopted individual initiates his embryonic return through pranayama and/or engages in a psychospiritual process of inquiry into his felt and lived-body experience, the intention is on integration, growth, and transformation. His child desires an authentic *thrice born* autonomy from the closed adoption system and the embodiment of spirit, despite that he is not sure where the womb from which he came from is located; he feels as if he never was even born. Thus, the womb becomes a forbidden, lost place, the condition of having been born becomes lost. Without the original birth certificate, there is no proof (Lifton, 1994).

Adopted person and writer Axness (2012) explained that part of the adult adopted person's journey of returning to the womb is about experiencing the lived experience of a conception that wasn't intended. This lived experience for adopted individuals carries a great sense of recognition and relief because the contextual patterns locked in the body are unraveled with empathic self-parental mirroring. When the experience and felt sense can be restructured in the body's container, making the body a strong and autonomous vehicle for spirit and soul, feelings of mutual connection with other human beings and the illumination of the "real self" can gradually be restored (Bernhardt, 1992, as cited in Bentzen, et al., 2004).

The return to the shadow of the womb, which qualifies as the first dark shadow the child experiences and that which continues to feel as if it is swallowing the child, signifies the adopted person's return to the unknown and dark chthonian Great Mother. The dark womb is mysterious and holds the potential secrets of his blood and identity. Vessels—such as a cave, dwelling, tent, temple—lie at the core of the elementary character of the Feminine (Neumann, 1963). Seen in this way, traveling back to the womb is like the Greek goddess Persephone traveling to the dark unknown underworld to meet Hades—the primordial Dark Lord. Stein (2006) reflected:

> ... for Persephone is an aspect of every person, male or female, and her ravishment is the relation of the individuated soul to a darkly numinous background that is the shadow of death itself, the overwhelming character of an aspect of Being that, though beyond identity, is still irrevocably intimate with what one is. (p. 89)

If the perpetual child's soul is like Persephone, then to be violated by this vast dark figure from the underground has a possible parallel transformation in each of us. This transformation resemblances other initiations in the details of certain birth and funeral rites (van Gennep, 1960). The Feminine is usually associated with the cycle of birth, death, and rebirth.

Transformation and change in the embryonic stage is ultimately about the mysteries of the Feminine. As in any transformative process, there are stages. For the mysteries of the Feminine, they are divided into: preservation, formation, nourishment, and transformation (Neumann, 1963). The stages of the mysteries of the Feminine parallel the phases of initiations and rites of passages—separation, transition, and incorporation. They also mirror the stages of psychospiritual development that the perpetual child must undergo in order for the spirit and flesh to join. The adopted child continues to face the dark Mother's womb but in an external form for the next phase of development.

Jungian analyst and writer Neumann (1990) explained that there are two embryonic phases in which the whole first year of infancy must be assimilated to the embryonic phase. The first phase, and the one which is often neglected by child development, is where the child is still psychically and physically integrated with the mother's body. The child is participating in a *participation mystique* that demonstrates the quality of union or merger that characterizes the mother-child relationship in this earliest period of infancy. The child also has an *unconscious identity*. Because the mother-child relationship is so bonded at this stage, the mythological image of the snake with its tail in its mouth—the uroboros—signifies this phase of development. The strong bonds of connection are contributed to the human infant being born approximately a year early in comparison to the maturity at birth of other higher primates. To achieve a comparable degree of maturity at birth the infant would probably have to spend at least another year in the womb.

The second phase in the embryonic gestational period is when the child has entered into human society and its ego and consciousness begin to develop and grow into the language and customs of its group. Archetypal development then begins in the nurturing, protective atmosphere of the womb and then, following birth, continues in the *social womb*. The adopted child is at an immediate disadvantage within the social womb because the only language and customs the closed adoption group creates are the rhythms and rituals of secrecy and silence. Rites or initiations are not performed to mark the child's separation and autonomy from mother, who is symbolized as the primal Great Mother.

Before the comprehensive human *figure* of the Great Mother appeared, the still-unformed image arose with innumerable symbols—particularly nature symbols from every realm of nature. Gradually, they became linked with the attributes of the Great Mother and form the wreath of symbols that surround the archetypal figure in rites and myths (Neumann, 1963). van Gennep (1960) wrote that rites performed by indigenous man recognized the separation from the mother by passing the child's body through, across, or under something, and putting the child on the ground. This signifies a rite of incorporation with Mother Earth, also known as the "Mistress of the Plants" (Neumann, 1990, p. 112). She is the goddess of growth and nourishment. Even the child's umbilical cord itself is handled through rites of passages. The dark womb matter is placed with care and is buried in the earth in order for the child's flesh and soul to grow as one.

In the social womb of closed adoptions, the dark primal womb substance that comes from the Great Mother's body is left in the hands of the closed adoption system that promotes a fundamentally artificial birthing process; nothing is natural about it. The unnatural attitudes and lack of initiation and rites of passages are at a very far distance from Mother Earth—she is autonomous, healing, and naturally beautiful, the closed system is not. Thus, the adopted child cannot take into his body the Great Mother who is attuned to the natural growth of her child and to his "times" (Neumann, 1990, p. 114) which, like the tides, are determined by an—unconscious—lunar rhythm. The lunar rhythm symbolizes the feminine and the movement of the body's container.

The lunar cycle is also associated with the feminine blood. As previously stated, whether he knows it or not, the child's mother's menstruation affects his life (Shuttle & Redgrove, 1986). At some level in the unconscious, the adopted child knows and feels her flow of blood in his body but cannot fully comprehend and appreciate its force. The Great Mother's body and blood feels like it is lost forever to the child. The ritual and rhythm of life then, which accent, preserve and raise to consciousness the natural divisions of day and night feel like the old splits and holes in the psyche and body. The adult adopted individual must be on constant watch then for any hints as to the whereabouts of the Great Mother in his own blood, rhythm, and genetic ties. The Great Mother's blood is gone but he can reclaim it in initiatory conceptions.

## Initiation of Adoption: Reclaiming the Story

*There is no ritual ceremony, like lighting candles or sitting shivah, to mourn parents who are as if dead, while never having been as if legitimately alive* (Lifton, p. 41).

Coming full circle like the uroboros snake that represents the ever-connected bond between mother, the Great Mother, and her child, the adopted adult has the lifelong initiatory process and journey of separating from the complex of the mother archetype, making the transition to a new kin group, and incorporating and integrating the experience into a coherent sense of self and identity. This life is truly the path of individuating and breaking apart from the confining limitations of the closed adoption's entrapment; she is becoming an autonomous adult. Although grueling, the perpetual child is then not only *twice born* but *thrice born* when the adult adopted person initiates a series of intentional and conscious initiatory conceptions on her path.

Hand in hand with this process is the withdrawal of the spirit from the mother to the person of the child, a development with whose completion the earliest form of child autonomy is achieved; it is with this formation of a unitary Self that the human child is truly born (Neumann, 1990). Similarly, life does not begin at conception for the adopted child, or at the moment he emerges from the womb and gives his first outraged cry but at the moment he is told about being adopted. "Adoption is the birth of consciousness, the consciousness of being different from the people around him" (Lifton, p. 21). The child's ego is split.

Despite adoption's birth of a split consciousness,

there are no rites of passages that involve a direct rite of assimilation into the new kin group. Severson (1994) stated,

> On other great occasions, when so much is at stake and transformations are so complete, it has been the way of humankind to ritually mark it with a toast, a feast, with sacred words and public celebration. But at the moment of an adoptive placement, no such ritual occurred, perhaps because of our collective wish to pretend that nothing had really happened, that being adopted or belonging to an adoptive family was identical with being born and raised by one's own kind, one's own people, one's own 'blood kin.' (p. 22)

Without conscious initiations and rites of passages to recognize the adopted child's adoption, no one can question or wonder why the perpetual child does not grow up; she has not grown up because she never existed.

Furthermore, Neumann (1990) stated, "Loss of the mother or of the person substituting for her is felt less in the bodily than in the psychic sphere" (pg. 20). However, the adopted adult doesn't have the story about his adoption later on to make sense of his body experiences; engagement in initiatory conceptions needs the body as a tool and vehicle for the phases of transition and integration. As stated earlier, images from the closed adoption system are dark and silent but can creatively be used when the light of consciousness is brought to them.

Engagement in meditation—such as *Samatha* meditation which can create a serene attentional state in which the hindrances of excitation and laxity have been thoroughly calmed (Wallace, 1999)—is one way in which a series of initiatory conceptions can be catalyzed . In *Samatha* meditation, an individual brings his attention to the in and out breath to quiet the mind or the practitioner can focus on the silence and *nothingness* between the thoughts and breaths. The discipline of *Samatha* is not bound to any one religious or philosophical creed. Other types of attentional trainings are found in varying extents in many of the contemplative traditions throughout history, including Hinduism, Buddhism, Taoism, Christianity and Sufism.

Meditation is just one form of initiatory practice and training that can help transition, integrate, and in turn *rebirth* the flesh and the spirit into one. Any images that arise from the experience of just noticing—a form of insight meditation called Vipassana—can be later processed and restructured in the body and included in the story and identity of one's life and existence. The idea then that the dark images of adoption can creatively and freely move through the adopted person's body towards a future "identity of possibility" (Leighton, 2005, p. 147) becomes feasible. Woodman (1982) reflected,

> While the laws of the world of matter (nature) are not the laws of the world of psyche (soul), the images apply to both worlds; they are the connectors. If we concentrate on the images in our stories and dreams until we distill their truth, we ground ourselves in the reality of our own imagery." p. 9)

The reality of the adopted child's dark imagery is birthed out of the closed adoption system.

The closed adoption system is the result of the patriarchal culture that the adopted individual grew up in and still lives in due to the denial of adult adopted person's being given their original birth certificates. No wonder then that adopted persons never grow up: They are not allowed to know the truth of their birthright. Joyce Pavao's tells a story about being referred to by a professional as an "adopted child" when Joyce was an adult! This highlights the problem. Even in others' eyes, the adopted adult has not grown up because the system gave the child unrealistic ideals of perfection--of what it means and feels like to be adopted. Invalidating messages such as you were chosen, picked, or special and that the adoption experience is no big deal (Brodzinsky et al., 1992) come at a heavy price for the *adopted adult child* that too few of persons in our society understand or care to recognize.

Stories such as the ones told to adopted individuals form incoherent narratives in our life stories. They invalidate true and authentic lived and embodied experiences; they invalidate a living life. Because the child does not know or understand better, the invalidating stories from the closed adoption system *feed from the child's spirit*, instead of *feeding the spirit*. Feeding the spirit entails a lot of heavy lifting and work later in life. Psychospiritual work and initiations can help with the burden of reconnecting our true stories to our bodies and spirits, while we keep in mind that the stories the child is holding onto are the ones that can later set her spirit free. An *earned security* later in life comes from feeling felt; initiatory and psychospiritual practices can help. "In essence... to 'feel felt'... Such a feeling of connection, in fact, may be extremely important for each of us in our relationships throughout the lifespan" (Siegel, 2001, p. 84).

Adoption expert Pavao (2005) reflected the importance of knowing one's true story about birth:

> Many adoptees feel as if they came from outer space because there is no story of their birth, only the wonderful story of their adoption. Each child also needs a story of his or her birth—a sense of a beginning and of being human. (p. 64)

Without our authentic birth stories, "we lack the

cosmos that keeps us in touch with the universal reality. Without stories, we have no way to recollect ourselves when our personal world shatters." (Woodman, 1992, p. 5). The perpetual child is lost in the closed system and has no way to be reached. Hence, initiations and rituals regarding our stories, births, and spirit are vital in recognizing and meeting the child's Essence, spirit, and soul in the adult's flesh.

## Initiation of Search and Reunion

*All people who walk the face of the earth possess the inalienable right to know their history and to meet the man and woman from whom they drew life and breath* (Severson, 1991, p. 105).

When adopted individuals set out on the search for their biological kin, they are answering what mythologist and writer Joseph Campbell described as *The Call*—the first stage of the mythic journey in which the hero ventures forth from the familiar world into the unknown. As any adopted person has experienced in his search, the journey involves many initiatory conceptions all on its own; initiations and rites of passages are essentially embedded in the search and reunion process. The adopted person is venturing into the stages of separation, transition, and integration. Feelings about loss, identity, and ambiguity get stirred up as one chooses to cross over the threshold into the unknown, mysterious, and foreign landscape.

Many writers such as Brodzinsky, et al. (1992), Lifton (1983, 1994) Pavao (2005) Schooler (1995), Sorosky, et al. (1984) and Strauss (1994) have all vividly recalled and described antidotal accounts of the search and reunion process for adopted individuals. So many accounts echo similarities between search and reunion and initiations and rites of passages. One example is Lifton's (1994) description about search being a *quest* of coming to terms with one's identity, power, will, and destiny:

> The journey is the adoptee's heroic attempt to bring together the split parts of the self. It is an authentic way of being born again. It is an act of will; a new dimension of experience. It is the quest of the intrinsic nature one was born with before it got twisted out of shape by secrecy and disavowal. It is a way of modifying the past, of living out the script that might have been. It is a way of taking control of one's own destiny, of seizing power. It is a way of finding oneself. (p. 135)

The search is also as Pavao (2005) wrote a time of distinct "normative crisis." (p. 75). It is a crisis between what feels at times like the inexorable battle between the split parts, body, and spirit.

At the beginning of the initiatory conception, *The Call* to search is usually triggered by an intense experience such as marriage, parenthood, death of adoptive parents, psychotherapy, etc. (Sorosky, et al., 1984). "Sometimes it is the search that is an end in itself, for it provides the adoptee with an outlet for his/her frustrations" (Sorosky, et al., 1984, p. 156). The search to others is an outlet for healing. Filmmaker and writer Strauss (1994) recalled that her search meant "a big step toward healing. It is an acknowledgment, whether conscious or subconscious, that a deep and profound loss exists, which requires attention" (p. 324). Loss again resurfaces on the adopted person's path and reflects the initial stage of separation of the initiation and rite of passage.

*The Call* to search originates from the child's spirit to find the feeling point of contact with the loss and separation, thus revitalizing a dormant series of initiatory conceptions of psychospiritual growth and development; feelings in the body give away clues. Severson's (1994) honed in on the feelings of this loss with the notion of *comfort of kinship*. *Comfort of kinship* is to be and feel inextricably interconnected, to maintain a sense that we are watched over and cared about by those who have come and gone on before us, to believe that not only here in this life but through the generations the circle is unbroken and yields a profound sense of comfort. "One place where the comfort of kinship will probably never be found is in the autobiography of an adoptee" (p. 179). One clearly feels the sense of loss here for the adopted individual. Where in the body does the adopted individual sense this loss and can the perpetual child help the adult adopted person breath the light of spirit into this recognized place in the body?

## Conclusion

In any process and path of psychospiritual development and growth, one comes back to the original series of initiatory conceptions and rites of passages to complete the full cycle of transition and incorporation; as depicted in the image of the uroboros snake. The separation from search and reunion has been activated so what stage is next? Transpersonal writer Washburn (1995) offered some clues in his transpersonal perspective on human development. He wrote, "The period of regressive deconstruction is over and the ego enters a period of healing reconstruction, a period that, adopting traditional terminology, I shall call *regeneration of spirit*" (Washburn, 1995, p. 203).

In general, a *regeneration of spirit* consists of a psychospiritual deconstruction followed by a period of radical psychic reconstruction. Translated, the deconstruction can be seen as the separation stage in a series of initiations and rites of passages that the adopted individual undergoes along the adoption path; the search for the true self and identity is a deconstruction as well as a reconstruction and regeneration of spirit. The initiations along the path of birth, adoption, and search and reunion demonstrate the psychospiritual potential of development, transformation, and growth. The stage of transition in these initiations is when the deconstructed container—one that could be shattered by the disillusionment of the closed adoption system—is slowly mended and consequently strengthened for a reconstruction of a new life, identity, and body to be breathed in by the light of spirit.

Reflecting this strength are those women in the author's dissertation research who appeared to fare better to the storms of the closed adoption system when they engaged in some series of psychospiritual initiatory conceptions. In turn, they had a quicker transition time from the separation stage and were more able to connect with the deepest base of the psyche. They chose practices that were unique and individual to them, although every one of them had a common thread—they had some form of deep contemplation, meditation, yoga, and/or creativity to them. As a result of these women's different psychospiritual practices, they felt better equipped to explore the many initiations on their adoption path. They had undergone an initiation of being *thrice born* and their spirits were in sync with their flesh. One co-researcher stated that she felt "whole," another woman said she was "a survivor," and most women displayed empathy for their adoptive parents and first/birth parents. They blamed the misguidance and negligence of the closed adoption system.

Overall, adult adopted women who presented coherent narratives about their adoption stories, empathy for others, and compassion for themselves demonstrated integration of mind, body, and spirit. *Integration* is an inherited destiny belonging to the human race as a whole (Washburn, 1995). Integration is also the basic process of the development of the mind, emotional well-being, and psychological resilience throughout the lifespan. It creates a core-self experience that is coherent and feels inherently connected to others (Siegel, 2001). Adopted adult women who engaged in initiatory conceptions demonstrated integration.

Furthermore, during initiations and rites of passages, the body is "resurrected" (Washburn, 1995, p. 231) during regression for the service of transcendence and then the ego is "reincarnated" (Washburn, 1995, p. 231) during regeneration in spirit. The transformation causes the person to feel their authentic feelings without getting swept away by them. Ultimately transformation happens when an individual can embrace her full adoptive identity while also being able to let go and not be attached and swallowed up by it.

One common mistake in the integration phase for adopted individuals, however, is continuing to regress back to the unborn status and separation, consequently the child getting stuck in deciphering between the mother and the Great Mother. The child has little knowledge and understanding of the two because the closed adoption system has not honored or recognized either one's spirit in initiations. Jungian analyst Neumann (1990) stated,

> The mother constellates the archetypal field and evokes the archetypal image of the mother in the child psyche, where it rests, ready to be evoked and to function. This archetypal image evoked in the psyche then sets in motion a complex interplay of psychic functions in the child, which is the starting point for essential psychic developments between the ego and the unconscious (p. 24).

On the other hand, one must keep in mind that the "good Great Mother" (Neumann, 1990, p. 21) is anonymous and transpersonal, in other words archetypal, as the one part of a specifically human constellation which operates between her and the child. Her unconsciously directed behavior, which enables her to coincide with the mother archetype, is vitally necessary to the normal development of the child.

Severson (1994) highlights the confusion between mother and the archetypal Great Mother in his critique of Nancy Verrier's (1993) *Primal Wound* theory. Verrier popularly termed that the adopted person experiences trauma when she is relinquished by her first/birth mothers. Although the current author was very resistant at first to disclaim and call into question Verrier's theory, I began to open up to the possibility of an alternative view because I observed how stuck and identified my child was with this view; I was too emotionally attached and somatically triggered by it. By disidentifying from my emotional reaction and engaging in a series of initiatory conceptions with meditation and contemplation, I realized that Severson was pointing me toward a different reality that perhaps fit better with my adoption experience now. I was continuing to move forward toward transformation and growth on my adoption path.

Also pertinent to the discussion is Severson's critique about Verrier's *Primal Wound* theory that it is "psychologically naïve" (Severson, 1994, p. 96). He explained that the idea draws resonance and is *self-evident* in nature by virtue of the fact that it expresses an *archetypal* idea or image. The theory is in the grip of the Mother-Child archetype. By archetypal, Severson means that it is a universal recurring image, occurring cross-culturally, with great emotional appeal. In and of itself, the archetypal image is one that begs to elicit an initiatory conception. Thus, the psychological and philosophical task is to "consciously integrate it, which is not synonymous with "rationalization," (Severson, 1994, p. 97) so that one remains sensitive to other ideas, other images, other values which may have an equal relevance to the experience one is imagining and investigating.

Instead of offering insights, Verrier (1993) is proposing an ideology. What we are talking about in the proposed ideology of the *Primal Wound* is about "the big M and the big F—Mother complex and Father complex, the two biggest dynamos in our psyches" (Woodman, 1992, p. 12). However, the archetype of the mother in the adopted adult can become autonomous and function like an independent organ. She can then manifest with all the transpersonal symbols and qualities characteristic of the archetype—not merely of the personal mother who releases it (Neumann, 1990).

Bonding or lack of bonding to our personal parents generates these dynamos of unconscious association that influence our future relationship with men, women, children, and society. The adopted individual's perpetual child may not have felt connected or bonded because of the holes and splits that the closed adoption system left in its wake. His umbilical cord may still be connected to male values (the father's or mother's or both) that feels like his very survival depends upon obeisance to the patriarchal standards of the closed system; his body, spirit, and soul feel weak. Thus, engagement in conscious and intentional initiations on the adoption path to consummate the flesh and spirit is crucial for the perpetual child to grow up.

An initiation and rite of passage for severing the umbilical cord from the closed adoption system can help clarify that the relationship to the archetype is complex and any emotional disturbances in the primal relationship with the Great Mother have nothing to do with blood kinship, for the true mother is more or less replaceable by a figure playing an analogously affective role. In other words, it is not the personal individual, but the generically maternal in each of us—which is difficult for the adopted individual to recognize and attune his bodily rhythms with due to them being lost in closed adoption system—that is the indispensable foundation of the child's life (Neumann, 1990).

Regardless of our genes being lost, autonomy is possible when the adopted individual engages in a series of initiatory conceptions and practices that evoke psychospiritual development on his or her adoption path; the perpetual child will be re-mothered regardless of which parent is present because the light of consciousness will be present. Overall, conscious and intentional initiations can help move the process of psychospiritual process along for the perpetual child in a direction toward healing, growth, and transformation. The perpetual child can be thrice, fourth, and however many times *reborn* in order to transform and grow up.

# References

Almaas, A., H. (1987). *Diamond heart book one: Elements of the real man.* Boston, MA: Shambala.

Anderson, R. (2000). Intuitive inquiry: Interpreting objective and subjective data. *ReVision, 22*(4), 31-39.

Axness, M. (2012). *Parenting for Peace: Raising the next generation of peacemakers.* Boulder, CO: Sentient.

Bentzen, M., Jarlnaes, E., Levine, P. (2004). The body self in psychotherapy: A psychomotoric approach to developmental psychology. In I. Macnaughton (Ed.), *Body, breath, & consciousness: A somatics anthology: A collection of articles on family systems, self-psychology, the bodynamics model of somatic developmental psychology, shock trauma, and breathwork* (pp. 51-70). Berkeley, CA: North Atlantic.

Brodzinsky, D. M., Schechter, M. D., Henig, R. M. (1992). *Being adopted: The lifelong search for self.* New York, NY: Anchor.

Caplan, M. (2009). *Eyes wide open: Cultivating discernment on the spiritual path.* Boulder, CO: Sounds True.

Eliade, M., & Meade, M. (2009). *Rites and symbols of initiation: The mysteries of birth and rebirth.* Spring Publications.

Eliade, M. (1990). *Yoga: Immortality and freedom.* Princeton, NJ: PUP.

Estes, C. P. (2012, April). Adoption and destiny. *Keynote Address.* Workshop conducted at the meeting of the American Adoption Congress, Denver, CO.

Feldman, C. (2005). *Woman awake: Women practicing Buddhism.* Berkeley, CA: Rodmell Press. Jaggard, S. I. (2001). The adoption puzzle: Bringing pieces together at mid-life. *Dissertation Abstracts International.* (UMI No. 9999045).

Johnson, D. H. (1992). *Body: Recovering our sensual wisdom.* Berkeley, CA: North Atlantic Books.

Kabat-Zinn, J. (1990). *Full catastrophe living: Using the wisdom of your body and mind to face stress, pain, and illness.* New York, NY: Delacorte.

Kabat-Zinn, J. (1994). *Wherever you go, there you are: Mindfulness meditation in everyday life.* New York, NY: Hyperion.

Kabat-Zinn, J. (2009). Foreword. In F. Didonna (Ed.), *Clinical Handbook of Mindfulness* (pp. xxv-xxxiii). New York, NY: Springer.

Leighton, K. (2005). Being adopted and being a philosopher:

Exploring identity and the "desire to know" differently. In S. Haslanger & C. Witt (Eds.), *Adoption matters: Philosophical and feminist essays* (pp. 146-170). Ithaca, NY: Cornell University.

Lewis, D. (1997). *The tao of natural breathing: For health, well-being, and inner growth.* San Francisco, CA: Mountain Wind.

Lifton, B. J. (1983). *Lost and found: The adoption experience.* NY, NY: Dial.

Lifton, B. J. (1994). *Journey of the adopted self: A quest for wholeness.* NY, NY: Basic Books.

Marrone, R. (1990). *Body of knowledge: An introduction to body/mind psychology.* New York, NY: SUNY.

Mindell, A. (1985). *Working with the dreaming body.* London, England: Arkana.

Neumann, E. (1963). *The great mother: An analysis of the archetype.* Princeton, NJ: PUP.

Neumann, E. (1990). *The child.* Boston, MA: Shambala.

Pavao, J. M. (2005). *The family of adoption:* Boston, MA: Beacon.

Rosen, R. (2002). *The yoga of breath: A step-by-step guide to pranayama.* Boston, MA: Shambala.

Schooler, J. (1995). *Searching for a past: The adopted adult's unique process of finding identity.* Colorado Springs, CO: Pinon.

Sorosky, A. D., Baran, A., Pannor, R. (1984). *The*

*adoption triangle: Sealed or open records: How they affect adoptees, birth parents, and adoptive parents.* Las Vegas, NV: Triadoption.

Severson, R. W. (1991). *Adoption: Charms and rituals for healing.* Dallas, TX: House of Tomorrow.

Severson, R. W. (1994). *Adoption: Philosophy and experience.* Dallas, TX: House of Tomorrow.

Severson, R. (1979). Puer's wounded wing: Reflections on the psychology of skin  disease. In J. Hillman (Ed.), *Puer papers* (pp. 129-151). Dallas, TX: Spring.

Shuttle, P., Redgrove, P. (1986, revised ed). *The wise wound: Myths, realities, and meanings of menstruation.* New York, NY: Grove.

Siegel, D. J. (2001). Toward an interpersonal neurobiology of the developing mind: Attachment relationships, "mindsight," and neural integration. *Infant Mental Health Journal, 22*(1-2), 67-94.

Stein, C. (2006). *Persephone unveiled: Seeing the goddess & freeing your soul.* Berkeley, CA: North Atlantic.

Stauss, J. A. S. (1994). *Birthright: The guide to search and reunion for adoptees, birthparents, and adoptive parents.* New York, NY: Penguin.

Topfer. A. (2010). Psychospiritual development of female adoptees raised within a closed adoption system: A theoretical model within a feminist and Jungian perspective. *International Journal of Transpersonal Psychology, 29*(2), pp. 87-102.

van Gennep, A. (1960). *The rites of passage.* Chicago, IL: UCP.

Verrier, N. (1993). *The primal wound: Understanding the adopted child.* Baltimore, MA: Gateway.

von Franz, L. (1981, Second ed.). *Puer aeternus.* Boston, MA: Sigo.

Wallace, A., B. (1999). The Buddhist tradition of samatha: Methods for refining and examining consciousness. *Journal of Consciousness Studies,* 6(2–3), 175–187.

Washburn, M. (1995). *The ego and the dynamic ground: A transpersonal theory of human development.* Albany, NY: SUNY.

Woodman, M. (1982). *Addiction to perfection: The still unravished bride.* Toronto, Canada: Inner City.

Woodman, M. (1992). *Leaving my father's house: A journey to conscious femininity.* Boston, MA: Shambhala.

Zweig, C. (Ed.) (1990). *To be a woman: The birth of the conscious feminine.* New York, NY: Putnam.

# Contributor Biographies

## PERPETUAL CHILD: AN ADULT ADOPTEE ANTHOLOGY

### DISMANTLING THE STEREOTYPE

**Laura Dennis**

LAURA DENNIS is an adult adoptee in reunion with her maternal biological family. Born in New Jersey, raised in Maryland, she considers herself a "California girl," even though she currently lives in her husband's hometown, Belgrade, Serbia, with their two small children. *Adopted Reality*, Laura's 9/11 memoir of adoption, reunion and a brief bout with insanity is available on Amazon. She blogs at www.laura-dennis.com

**Mei-Mei Akwai Ellerman**

Born and adopted in the United States, Dr. Ellerman received her doctorate at Harvard, and studied at Boston University, the University of Geneva, and the Liceo Classico Michelangiolo in Florence. After three decades of teaching Italian literature and cinema at Boston area institutions, Mei-Mei now focuses on research, writing, social activism and reiki practice. She is a scholar at the Brandeis Women's Studies Research Center where she pursues her combined interests. A founding board director of the Polaris Project [leading anti-human trafficking NGO in the US based in Washington, DC, and operator of the sole National Human Trafficking Hotline and Resource Center], as emerita, Mei-Mei remains deeply committed to combating modern-day slavery and fundraising for Polaris. She also serves on the board of Chinese Adoptee Links International and Global Generations and contributes regularly to the ChineseAdoptee.com blog. Recent participation in Adoption conferences has led her to increased involvement in the fight against fraudulent adoption practices and for universal access to their personal records by all adopted individuals.

Since 2004 Mei-Mei has been a member of the International Advisory Board of the A.G. Bell Association for the Deaf and Hard of Hearing. Her life-long interest in the deaf stems from growing up with her two maternal aunts who came to the United States from China in the early 1900s to attend the Clarke School for the Deaf in Northampton, MA.

Mei-Mei is currently working on two memoirs, both of which have involved worldwide research and travel. *Circles of Healing, Circles of Love: A Labyrinthine Journey in Search of Connection*, the daunting 27-year-long quest for her Chinese biological origins, has led her to China six times as she has painstakingly unraveled the mystery surrounding her birth and the complex legal barriers put in place to thwart any investigatory attempts. *In Pursuit of Images and Shadows: A Chinese Daughter's Pilgrimage into her Mother's Past,* is a cultural biography covering 160 years of her bi-racial adoptive family history. It draws upon personal narratives, letters, and photographs dating back to the late 1800s, interwoven with discoveries made in the course of years of global research. Travels to

Denmark, China, Thailand, Korea, and Australia among other destinations, have allowed the author to solve long-held family secrets and reassess vital aspects of her Danish grandfather's career (Commissioner for over 40 years of the Chinese Imperial Maritime Customs, and Danish Ambassador to China). They have also yielded the keys to unlock the mystifying past of her Chinese grandmother.

Links:
www.chineseadoptee.com
www.PolarisProject.org

National Human Trafficking Hotline
and Resource Center:
1-888-3737-888
www.brandeis.edu/wsrc/about/index.html
www.listeningandspokenlanguage.org/Who_We_Are/

## Lynn Grubb

LYNN was born and adopted in Illinois in the 1960s and was raised and currently lives in Dayton, Ohio, with her husband of 22 years, Mark, and their two children (one by birth and one by adoption). Lynn holds a bachelors degree from Wright State University and a paralegal certificate from the American Institute of Paralegal Studies. She is the Policy Columnist for *Lost Daughters* and is on the legislative committee of the Adoptee Rights Coalition. Lynn is a former Court Appointed Special Advocate (CASA) and is passionate about writing from a place of authenticity. Please visit her at: www.noapologiesforbeingme.blogspot.com

## Lee Herrick

LEE HERRICK is the author of *Gardening Secrets of the Dead* (WordTech Editions, 2012) and *This Many Miles from Desire* (WordTech Editions, 2007). His poems have been published widely in literary magazines and anthologies, including The Bloomsbury Review, ZYZZYVA, Berkeley Poetry Review, Highway 99: A Literary Journey Through California's Great Central Valley, 2nd edition, Seeds from a Silent Tree: Writing by Korean Adoptees, and Indivisble: Poems for Social Justice, among others. He guest edited New Truths: Writing in the 21st Century by Korean Adoptees, and his narrative essay, "What Is This Thing Called Family?" appears in university textbooks. He has traveled throughout Latin America and Asia, and he has given readings throughout the United States. He was born in Daejeon, South Korea, adopted at ten months old, and raised in the East Bay and later, Central California. He lives with his daughter and wife in Fresno, California, where he teaches at Fresno City College and in the low-residency MFA Program at Sierra Nevada College. www.leeherrick.com

## Jennifer Bao Yu "Precious Jade" Jue-Steuck

Born to a birthmother from Jiangsu Province, China, Jennifer is from Laguna Beach (OC), California. She studied comparative literature and creative writing for film at New York University's *Tisch School of the Arts*, under the direction of Sam Pollard, and completed her masters at Harvard University (Jane Fonda's *Gender Studies Program*) as a *Bill & Melinda Gates Foundation Scholar*. She is the founder of Chinese Adoptee Links (CAL) International, the first global grassroots group created by and for the more than 150,000 Chinese adoptees of all ages in 26 countries, and is co-founder of *One World: Chinese Adoptee Links Blog* (www.ChineseAdoptee.com).

Jennifer has been primarily based in London at the British Library for her Ph.D. research (University of California at Berkeley) on motherloss theories and Chinese adoptees in the UK, the USA and Spain. Her current creative projects include a children's novel, *The Golden Gates of Grand Central*, and a memoir inspired by her adoptive mother, *Inspiration Ice Cream*. www.InspirationIceCream.com

## Karen Pickell

KAREN PICKELL is an editor and columnist at *Lost Daughters*, a collaborative blog written by adopted women. She holds a Master of Arts in Professional Writing and serves as associate editor of the online literary journal *Flycatcher*, based in suburban Atlanta where she lives. Karen also serves on the board of directors of the Georgia Writers Association and is an active member of the Georgia Poetry Society. She has previously published poetry and nonfiction, and is currently working on a memoir about her adoption experience. She blogs about writing, adoption, and other topics on *Between* at karenpickell.com

## Matthew Salesses

MATTHEW SALESSES was adopted at age two, returned to Korea as an adult, married a Korean woman, and writes a column about his wife and (biological) baby for *The Good Men Project*. He also serves as the Project's Fiction Editor. Matthew's essays and stories have been published in *The New York Times* Motherlode blog, *NPR*'s Code Switch, *Hyphen Magazine, Koream, Korean American Story, Glimmer Train, The Rumpus*, and elsewhere. He is currently a Ph.D. candidate at the University of Houston. His most recent book is a novel, *I'm Not Saying, I'm Just Saying* (Civil Coping Mechanisms), and his latest projects are a serialized illustrated novel to appear in the adoptee-run magazine, *Gazillion Voices*, and two eBooks forthcoming from Thought Catalog Books. www.matthewsalesses.com

*The Last Repatriate* was described by author and actor James Franco as "a subtly painful psychological journey" and was named to best of 2011 lists at Big Other and Heavy Feather.

## Nicky Sa-eun Schildkraut

NICKY SA-EUN SCHILDKRAUT is a writer of poetry and

prose, and teacher of college composition and creative writing who calls Los Angeles home. As a Korean adoptee (KAD), her creative and scholarly work reflects an ongoing interest to explore the emotional and historical aspects of the Korean diaspora as well as transnational adoption. Previously, she has collaborated on avant-garde music and art projects with music composers and visual artists. She holds an M.F.A. degree in poetry (2002) and a Ph.D. degree in Literature & Creative Writing from the University of Southern California (2012). She is currently completing a second book, lyrical and narrative poems inspired by transnational Asian cinema, and a non-fiction book about autopoetics and adoption narratives. Her debut collection of poetry *Magnetic Refrain* was released in February 2013 from Kaya Press.

### Lucy Chau Lai-Tuen Sheen

Made in Hong Kong exported to the UK in the late 50s early 60s as a transracial adoptee.

Brought up by a white family in the heartland of conservative England, next to the cucumber sandwiches, church spires and cricket on the village green.

Lucy trained at Rose Bruford College of Speech and drama.

Her first professional job was the female lead in the ground breaking British-Chinese feature film directed by Po Ch'ih Leong *PING PONG*. It achieved great critical acclaim in central Europe amongst the voices La Figaro and when it was presented at The Venice Film Festival.

Other film credits include *Business As Usual and Secrets & Lies*.

Lucy has worked extensively on stage, big and small screens, radio, multi-media, corporate training, presentation, commercials and as a drama support tutor.

Lucy has worked with and alongside some of the best British acting talent on offer, including Dame Helen Mirren

(Prime Suspect and The Queen) Eamonn Walker (Oz, Lights Out and Chicago Fire) Alexander Siddig (Star Trek Deep Space Nine) Roger Rees (The Life and Adventures of Nicholas Nickleby, Cheers, The West Wing, Warehouse 13) Pam Ferris (Matilda, Children of Men, Harry Potter) Kathryn Hunter (Harry Potter, Rome and Kafka's Monkey) and Hattie Morahan who is about to transfer to NY with the production of A Dolls House.

Theatre credits include *Riddley-* Walker-Exchange; *Julius Caesar*-Bristol Old Vic; *Drink the Mercury*-nominated for a TMA award; *Hungry Ghosts* by Tim Luscombe-nominated for an OFFIE. *Plenty*-directed by Thea Sharrock

TV credits include: *Prime Suspect 2; Eastenders; Lovejoy; Nighty Night Series 2.*

Radio credits include: *Words On A Night Breeze; Bound Feet and Western Dress.*

Lucy is now actively giving talks, lectures and presentations to and being asked to talk to a variety of professional organisations and groups active in the adoption field.

Lucy is also developing a relationship with The Mothers' Bridge of Love (www.mothersbridge.org) a charity founded and set up by the award winning author and journalist Xinran. This charity is here to help the many Chinese children adopted by western families, "to help the million overseas Chinese children who hardly understand their roots":

The Mothers' Bridge of Love helps to find answers to these questions by building a bridge:
* Between China and the rest of the world
* Between rich and poor
* Between birth culture and adoptive culture

It is hoped that Lucy will attend some of the many international conventions that Mothers' Bridge of Love and Xinran are present at and present a perspective from the point of view of an adult adoptee - something that is still even in the 21st century a rarity.

Lucy is currently developing several writing projects. She also writes under the name Lucy Chau Lai-Tuen. www.LucySheen.com

## Julie Stromberg

Born, adopted and raised in the Northeast United States, Julie reconnected with her natural parents and families in 1998. Since then, she has applied her lifelong experience as an adopted person to conducting critical analysis of global adoption practices.

Julie is a contributing board member of Pennsylvania Adoptee Rights. She writes about the adoptee experience as Co-Editor, Contributor, & Media Columnist of the collaborative blog of adopted women, Lost Daughters, and on her personal blog Life, Adopted.

An award-winning copywriter and digital content strategist, Julie holds a bachelor's degree in Journalism from Loyola University Maryland. Her essays on the adoption experience and industry have been published online and in print. When she isn't raising awareness about adoption reform, she is spending time with her husband and two sons--usually at basketball, lacrosse, or karate practice. www.juliestromberg.net

## April Topfer

APRIL TOPFER is a registered psychological assistant at the Mindful Center in Oakland, California where she specializes in adoption and uses mindfulness and mindful movement based on yoga as strategies with clients. She received her doctoral degree in Clinical Psychology from Sofia University (formerly known as the Institute of Transpersonal Psychology) in 2012. Her dissertation research explored adult adopted women's traditional and nontraditional mindfulness practices--yoga, journaling, meditation, swimming, creative expression--on their identities, adoption stories, and relationships. April also received her teacher yoga certification in 2013. April is currently President at PACER: Post-Adoption Center for Education and Research. PACER is a non-profit organization that serves all adoption triad members in Northern California with support groups. You can read more about April and her work at her website: www.mindfuladoptees.com

## Amanda H.L Transue-Woolston (co-editor)

AMANDA is a social worker, published author, and speaker. She has an A.A. in psychology, a B.S.W. in social work, and is currently a candidate for a master's in clinical social work. Amanda's work on adoption has appeared in multiple books, magazines, journal articles, radio interviews and has been presented at several conferences. She is a founding board member of the Adoption Policy and Reform Collaborative and also founded Pennsylvania Adoptee Rights and Lost Daughters. Amanda co-facilitates an adoption support group for anyone connected to adoption, and is a quarterly contributor to Gazillion Voices Magazine. Amanda is best known for her internationally recognized, award-winning adoption blog, The Declassified Adoptee.

## Angela Tucker

ANGELA TUCKER is a trans-racial adoptee, adopted from foster care - born in the South and raised in the Pacific Northwest. She recently reunited with some of her birth relatives, and is still actively searching for another birth sister. Angela holds a Bachelor's degree in Psychology and currently works at a university after spending several years working within domestic adoptions at a private adoption agency. Angela has delivered keynote speeches for adoption camps, fundraisers, birth parent retreats and other functions around the nation. Angela is married to Bryan Tucker, the documentarian and filmmaker of *Closure*; www.closuredocumentary.com, a feature length documentary that chronicles Angela's adoption search and reunion. She blogs about adoption, white privilege, race relations and cultural affairs at: www.theadoptedlife.com.

## Catana Tully

DR. CATANA TULLY was adopted as a baby by a German family in Guatemala in 1940. She grew up trilingual (German, Spanish, English) in Guatemala where she attended elementary and middle school. In tenth grade she entered an exclusive boarding school in Jamaica, WI and received her Advanced Level Higher Schools Certificate from Cambridge University, England. Expecting to become an international interpreter, she continued her studies at the Sprachen und Dolmetscher Institut in Munich, Germany. However, she was called to work in a play and discovered her affinity for the dramatic arts. She became the actress and fashion model Catana Cayetano and appeared in Film and TV work in Germany, Austria, and Italy. In Munich she met and married the American actor Frederick V. Tully and ultimately moved to the United States. They have a son, Patrick. In Upstate New York, she completed the BA in Cultural Studies, an MA in Latin American and Caribbean Literature, and a DA (doctor of Arts) in Humanistic Studies. She held the position of tenured Associate Professor at SUNY Empire State College, from which she retired in 2003. She returned in 2005 for part time work in ESC's Center for International Programs, where she served as Mentor and instructor in the Lebanon program, and as Interim Program Director for the Dominican Republic. In 2011 she retired completely to dedicate herself to publishing *Split at the Root: a Memoir of Love and Lost Identity*. Last spring semester the book was required reading as case study in USC's (University of Southern California) Master of Social Work program. The book is scheduled as required reading in spring 2014 for juniors majoring in English Lit. at Georgian Court University in NJ. Currently, *Split at the Root* is being translated into German and French.

A popular academic mentor, Dr. Catana Tully now makes use of her communicative skills as a dedicated coach who works with young and older adoptees who do not look like their parents, and parents who have or are planning to adopt interracially. She offers adoptees words of wisdom and tools to strengthen their impaired images of themselves, their race, their religion, and their culture. Learn more about her life and the book at: www.splitattheroot.com

## Diane René Christian (co-editor)

DIANE RENÉ CHRISTIAN is a short story writer and novelist. She is the author of *An-Ya and Her Diary (2012)* and founder of the *AN-YA Project*. Adoption has shaped Christian's life as the daughter to a step-parent adoptee, granddaughter to a domestic adoptee(US), and mom to two internationally adopted daughters. She was raised playing in the fields of Valley Forge Park and now resides in the Pacific Northwest. Learn more about the *AN-YA Project* at: www.anyadiary.com

16870636R00107